THE
COMPLETE
COOK

THE
COMPLETE
COOK

TIGER BOOKS INTERNATIONAL
LONDON

RECIPES COMPILED BY
Judith Ferguson

STYLED BY
Bridgeen Deery and Wendy Devenish

PHOTOGRAPHY BY
Peter Barry

DESIGNED BY
Philip Clucas, Sally Strugnell and Alison Jewell

2901
This edition published in 1994 by
Tiger Books International PLC, London
Text filmsetting by Inforum Typesetters, Portsmouth, Hants
Printed and bound in Singapore by Tien Wah Press.
All rights reserved
ISBN 1-85501-543-9

CONTENTS

INTRODUCTION

Creative cooking doesn't have to come from the kitchen of a top restaurant. Creative cooking doesn't have to involve expensive ingredients or time-consuming techniques. Creative cooking is perfectly possible at home using everyday ingredients. Some you'll find in your favourite supermarkets; some you'll find in any high street butchers, fishmongers or greengrocers.

Take a look around at fresh foods in their season and you'll find all the variety you could possibly want. The more often you look, the more familiar you'll be with the wealth of delicious and colourful ingredients you can use to brighten up meals, and with our recipes to inspire you, you'll soon have lots of ideas for creative ways to use them.

The Complete Home Cookbook draws on recipes from all over the world, but at the end of the day, the dishes are not so much exotic as adventurous. For instance, you'll find European, Asian, North American and even Mexican influences in many of the recipes in this book. However, we've taken just a few elements from these recipes and combined them with everyday ingredients, so delicious results are easy to achieve.

Try Fisherman's Stew, a hearty soup as flavourful as its French cousin, but without the expensive shellfish. Surprise yourself by preparing Sweet and Sour Pork that's every bit as good as that from your favourite Chinese restaurant. Make a pound of peeled or frozen prawns go further by stirring them into a lively Provençale sauce that's also full of vegetables. Choose red peppers instead of green for Stuffed Peppers, and fill them with a savoury chicken mixture to make a change from rice. Use the red, ripe tomatoes of summer combined with mozzarella cheese, oranges and basil for a sunny and sensational salad.

Try cutting vegetables into long, thin ribbons and tossing them with herbs and chopped nuts. Add spaghetti to a rice pilaff for a completely different side-dish for meat or poultry. Make a sauce of cherries to serve with chicken breasts for a stylish dinner party dish. Add colour to a steamed pudding with cranberries, or add zest to grilled trout with home-made Red Pepper Preserves. These are just a few of the recipe ideas you'll find in the pages of *The Complete Home Cookbook*.

Eating should be a pleasure, even when you've only put together a quick lunch, supper or snack, so we've selected our recipes with that in mind. There are starters and dinner party dishes included, as well as simple family fare, quick salads and snacks, satisfying soups and scrumptious puddings and desserts. None of the recipes are beyond the realm of any good cook, especially not when you consider all the special help that goes along with each one.

Creative cooking is confident cooking. One way to gain the necessary confidence in your own ability and feel at ease in the kitchen is to use recipes that are well explained and easy to follow. Ours are both. The step-by-step style, with colour photographs to illustrate the most important techniques, is the next best thing to having a cookery teacher at your side in the kitchen! Because pictures often explain things much more clearly than words, methods that might sound complicated become simpler when you can actually see them. Each of our recipes also has other useful features which help make light work of creating interesting, varied meals.

The Cook's Notes at the end of each recipe are an invaluable addition. Consult them to learn how to substitute alternative ingredients for those that are difficult to find. If you're economising, there are suggestions for cheaper alternative ingredients. There are hints to make preparation easier, and different cooking techniques are explained. Serving ideas suggest accompaniments that complement the dish and make the most of it. Each recipe gives the time for preparation and cooking so you'll know before you start how long the dish will take to create – a big help when you're planning a menu.

Finally, there is a colour photograph of each finished recipe, so you'll see at the beginning what the dish will look like at the end – a real bonus when you're trying something new! With easy-to-follow recipes and photographs to guide you, you can have fun cooking and enjoy preparing the recipes as much as you and your guests or family will enjoy eating them.

1

SOUPS
&
STARTERS

pages 10-51

SERVES 4-6

FRENCH ONION SOUP

A rich, satisfying soup to serve as a
starter or light supper on a cool evening.

60g/2oz butter or margarine
900g/2lbs onions, peeled and thinly sliced
10ml/2 tsps sugar
Pinch salt and pepper
25g/1½ tbsps flour
5ml/1 tsp dried thyme
1.7 litres/3 pints brown stock
140ml/¼ cup dry white wine

Croûtes

12 2.5cm/1 inch slices French bread
15ml/1 tbsp olive oil
225g/8oz grated cheese

1. Melt the butter in a large saucepan over a moderate heat. Stir in the onions and add the sugar. Cook, un-covered, over low heat, stirring occasionally, for 20-30 minutes or until the onions are golden brown.

2. Sprinkle the flour over the onions and cook for 2-3 minutes. Pour on the stock and stir to blend the flour. Add salt, pepper and thyme and return the soup to low heat. Simmer, partially covered, for another 30-40 minutes. Allow the soup to stand while preparing the croûtes.

3. Brush each side of the slices of bread lightly with olive oil and place them on a baking sheet. Bake in a preheated oven, 160°C/325°F/Gas Mark 3, for about 15 minutes. Turn the slices over and bake for a further 15 minutes, or until the bread is dry and lightly browned.

4. To serve, skim fat from the soup and ladle soup into a tureen or individual soup bowls. Place the croûtes on top of

Step 1 Brown the onions in a large saucepan with butter and sugar.

Step 3 Brush both sides of bread with olive oil and bake until lightly browned.

Step 4 Place the croûtes on soup and sprinkle with cheese.

the soup and sprinkle over the grated cheese. Place the soup in a hot oven and bake for 10-20 minutes, or until the cheese has melted. Brown under a preheated grill, if desired, before serving.

Cook's Notes

Time
Preparation takes about 20 minutes. Cooking takes about 50-60 minutes – 40 minutes for the soup, 30 minutes for the croûtes and 10-20 minutes to melt the cheese.

Cook's Tip
The addition of sugar helps the onions to brown.

SERVES 6

CHICKEN STUFFED PEPPERS

Try a stuffing that is different from the usual meat
and rice one for lighter tasting peppers.

3 large green or red peppers
60g/4 tbsps butter or margarine
1 small onion, finely chopped
1 stick celery, finely chopped
1 clove garlic, crushed
3 chicken breasts, skinned, boned and diced
10ml/2 tsps chopped parsley
½ loaf of stale bread, made into crumbs
1-2 eggs, beaten
Salt and pepper
90g/6 tsps dry breadcrumbs

1. Cut the pepper in half lengthwise and remove the
cores and seeds. Leave the stems attached, if desired.

2. Melt the butter in a frying pan and add the onion,
celery, garlic and chicken. Cook over moderate heat until
the vegetables are softened and the chicken is cooked.
Add the parsley. Season with salt and pepper.

3. Stir in the stale breadcrumbs and add enough beaten
egg to make the mixture hold together.

4. Spoon filling into each pepper half, mounding the top
slightly. Place the peppers in a baking dish that holds
them closely.

5. Pour enough water down the side of the dish to come
about 1.25cm/½ inch up the sides of the peppers. Cover
and bake in a pre-heated 180°C/350°F/Gas Mark 4 oven
for about 45 minutes, or until the peppers are just tender.

6. Sprinkle each with the dried breadcrumbs and place
under a preheated grill until golden brown.

Step 1 Cut peppers in half and remove seeds and white core.

Step 4 Spoon filling into the pepper halves, mounding the top and smoothing out.

Step 5 Place peppers close together in a baking dish and carefully pour in about 1.25cm/½ inch water.

Cook's Notes

Time
Preparation takes about 30
minutes and cooking takes
about 45-50 minutes.

Variations
Use spring onions in place of
the small onion. Add chopped
nuts or black olives to the filling, if
desired.

Serving Ideas
Serve as a first course, either
hot or cold, or as a light lunch
or supper with a salad.

SERVES 8-10

MINESTRONE

Everyone's favourite Italian soup doesn't always
have to contain pasta. Our's substitutes potatoes
and is hearty enough to serve as a meal.

225g/8oz dried white cannellini beans
30ml/2 tbsps olive oil
1 large ham bone
1 onion, chopped
2 cloves garlic, crushed
4 sticks celery, sliced
2 carrots, diced
1 small head Savoy cabbage or 450g/1lb fresh spinach,
    well washed
120g/4oz French beans, cut into 2.5cm/1 inch lengths
225g/8oz tomatoes, peeled, seeded and diced
1 dried red chilli pepper (optional)
2.5 litres/5 pints water (or half beef stock)
Salt and pepper
1 sprig fresh rosemary
1 bay leaf
3 potatoes, peeled and cut into small dice
3 courgettes, trimmed and cut into small dice
15ml/1 tbsp chopped fresh basil
15ml/1 tbsp chopped fresh parsley
Grated Parmesan cheese
Salt and pepper

1. Place the beans in a large bowl, cover with cold water
and leave to soak overnight.

2. Heat the oil in a large stock pot and add ham bone,
onion and garlic. Cook until onion has softened but not
coloured. Add the celery, carrots, cabbage and green
beans. If using spinach, reserve until later.

3. Drain the beans and add them to the pot with the
tomatoes and the chilli pepper, if using. Add the water and
bring to the boil, skimming the surface as necessary. Add
the rosemary and bay leaf and simmer, uncovered, until
the beans are tender, about 1¼ hours.

4. Add the potatoes and cook for the further 20 minutes.

5. Add the courgettes and spinach and cook, skimming
the surface, about 20 minutes longer. Remove the ham
bone, rosemary and bay leaf and add basil and parsley.
Serve with Parmesan cheese.

Step 1 Soak
beans overnight
in enough water to
cover. They will
swell in size.

Step 3 Using a
metal spoon, skim
any fat from the
surface of the
soup as it cooks.

Cook's Notes

 Time
Preparation takes about 20
minutes plus overnight
soaking for the beans. Cooking takes
about 2 hours.

 Watchpoint
The beans must be
thoroughly cooked – it can be
dangerous to eat them insufficiently
cooked.

 Serving Ideas
If desired, cooked pasta may
be substituted for the potatoes
and added at the end of cooking time.

 Variation
Other varieties of white beans
may be used and canned
beans may also be used. If using
canned beans, add them with
courgettes and spinach. Other
vegetables such as broccoli, turnips,
leeks or quartered Brussels sprouts,
may be substituted.

SERVES 4

QUICK LIVER PÂTÉ

Liver sausage is lightly seasoned and smoked and can be smooth or coarse. It makes an "instant" pâté.

300g/11oz German liver sausage
60g/2oz melted butter, preferably unsalted
1 clove garlic, crushed
30ml/2 tbsps brandy (optional)
Salt and pepper
Salad cress and black olives for garnish

Step 2 To fill a piping bag easily, fold the top half down over your hand. Spoon the mixture to be piped inside and then fold the top half back up over it.

Step 1 Place the sausage in a bowl with the butter, brandy, garlic, salt and pepper, and beat until smooth.

Step 3 To pipe, twist the top of the piping bag closed and hold with one hand. Use one finger to brace and guide the nozzle and press the mixture down from the top.

1. Place the sausage in a bowl with the butter, brandy, if using, garlic, salt and pepper and beat until smooth. Alternatively, use a food processor.

2. Pour the mixture into a piping bag fitted with a rosette nozzle.

3. Choose a large serving dish or individual plates and pipe out several swirls of pâté. Garnish with sliced or whole black olives and salad cress.

Cook's Notes

Time
Preparation takes about 15 minutes with about 30 minutes chilling.

Cook's Tip
Always squeeze out the mixture from the top of the piping bag down to the nozzle. If the bag is held in the middle, the mixture will soften and melt or it will burst out of the top.

Serving Ideas
Serve with hot toast fingers or thin slices of buttered rye bread.

SERVES 4-6

SWEET CORN AND POTATO SOUP

Such a filling soup, this is really a
complete meal in a bowl.

6 medium potatoes, peeled
Chicken or vegetable stock
1 onion, finely chopped
30g/2 tbsps butter or margarine
15g/1 tbsp flour
120g/4oz cooked ham, chopped
4 ears fresh sweetcorn or about 120g/4oz canned or
    frozen sweetcorn
850ml/1½ pints milk
Salt and white pepper
Finely chopped parsley

Step 3 Pour the potato mixture onto the flour and ham gradually, stirring constantly until well blended.

Step 4 Remove the husks and silk from the ears of corn.

Step 4 Use a sharp knife to cut the kernels off the cobs.

1. Quarter the potatoes and place them in a deep sauce-pan. Add stock to cover and the onion, and bring the mixture to the boil. Lower the heat and simmer, partially covered, until the potatoes are soft, about 15-20 minutes.

2. Drain the potatoes, reserving 430ml/¾ pint of the cooking liquid. Mash the potatoes and combine with reserved liquid.

3. Melt the butter or margarine in a clean pan, add the ham and cook briefly. Stir in the flour and pour over the potato mixture, mixing well.

4. If using fresh sweetcorn, remove the husks and silk and, holding one end of the corn, stand the ear upright. Use a large, sharp knife and cut against the cob vertically from top to bottom just scraping off the kernels. Add the corn and milk to the potato mixture and bring almost to the boil. Do not boil the corn rapidly as this will toughen it. Add a pinch of salt and white pepper, and garnish with parsley before serving.

Cook's Notes

Time
Preparation takes about 25 minutes and cooking takes about 25-30 minutes.

Preparation
The soup may be prepared in advance up to adding the corn. Bring the mixture to a rapid boil, turn down the heat and then add the corn and continue with the recipe. This soup does not freeze well.

Cook's Tip
When cooking sweetcorn on its own or adding it to other ingredients, add the salt just before serving. Cooking sweetcorn with salt toughens it.

SERVES 2-4

CREAMY DRESSED CRAB

This makes a delicious warm weather salad for
lunches, light suppers or elegant starters.

2 small crabs, boiled
30ml/2 tbsps oil
4 spring onions
1 small green pepper, seeded and finely chopped
1 stick celery, finely chopped
1 clove garlic, crushed
180ml/6 fl oz prepared mayonnaise
15ml/1 tbsp mild mustard
Dash tabasco and Worcestershire sauce
1 piece canned pimento, drained and finely chopped
30ml/2 tbsps chopped parsley
Salt and pepper
Lettuce

1. To shell the crabs, first remove all the legs and the large claws by twisting and pulling them away from the body.

2. Turn the shell over and, using your thumbs, push the body away from the flat shell. Set the body aside.

3. Remove the stomach sack and the lungs or dead man's fingers and discard them. Using a small teaspoon, scrape the brown body meat out of the flat shell.

4. Using a sharp knife, cut the body of the crab in four pieces and using a pick or a skewer, push out all the meat.

5. Crack the large claws and remove the meat in one piece if possible. Crack the legs and remove the meat as well, leaving the small, thin legs in the shell. Set all the meat aside. Scrub the shells if desired to use for serving.

6. Heat the oil in a small sauté pan or frying pan. Chop the white parts of the spring onions and add to the oil with the green pepper, celery and garlic. Sauté over gentle heat for about 10 minutes, stirring often to soften the vegetables but not brown them. Remove from the heat and set aside. When cool, add the mayonnaise, mustard, tabasco, Worcestershire sauce, pimento and finely chopped tops of the spring onions.

7. Spoon the reserved brown body meat from the crabs back into each shell or serving dish. Mix the remaining crab meat with the dressing, reserving the crab claws for garnish, if desired. They may also be shredded and added to the other crab meat. Do not overmix the sauce as the crab meat should stay in large pieces. Spoon into the shells on top of the brown body meat, sprinkle with chopped parsley and place the crab shells on serving plates, surrounding them with lettuce leaves, if desired. Garnish with the shelled crab claws and use the crab legs if desired. Sprinkle with parsley and serve immediately.

Step 3 Discard the plastic-like stomach sack and spongy lungs. Remove brown body meat from the shell of the crab and reserve it.

Step 4 Cut through the body of the crab with a sharp knife and pick out the crab meat with a skewer.

Cook's Notes

Time
Preparation takes about 45 minutes, cooking takes about 10 minutes.

Variation
If desired, recipe can be prepared with dressed or frozen crab meat. Allow about 90-120g/3-4 oz crab meat per person.

SERVES 6-8

CREAM OF PUMPKIN SOUP

For Halloween or Bonfire
Night this makes a warming
soup that's fun to serve.

1 large pumpkin about 2-2.5kg/4-5lbs in weight
60g/4 tbsps butter or margarine
1 large onion, sliced
280ml/½ pint double cream
Pinch salt, white pepper and nutmeg
Snipped chives to garnish

1. Wash the pumpkin well on the outside and cut around the stem, about 5cm/2 inches away from it.

2. Carefully cut most of the pulp off the top and reserve the "lid" for later use.

3. Remove the seeds from the inside and discard them.

4. Using a small, sharp knife, carefully remove all but 1.25cm/½ inch of the pulp from inside the pumpkin. Work slowly and carefully to avoid piercing the outer skin of the pumpkin. You can use a metal spoon if that proves easier. Chop all the pulp from the top of the pumpkin and the inside and set it aside.

5. Melt the butter or margarine in a large saucepan and add the onion. Cook slowly until the onion is tender but not brown. Add the pumpkin flesh and about 1150ml/2 pints cold water. Bring to the boil and then allow to simmer gently, covered, for about 20 minutes.

6. Purée the mixture in a food processor or blender in several small batches. Return the soup to the pot and add the cream, salt, pepper and nutmeg to taste. Reheat the soup and pour it into the reserved pumpkin shell. Garnish the top of the soup with snipped chives, if desired, before serving.

Step 2 Using a large, sharp knife, cut the top off the pumpkin to serve as a lid.

Step 3 Remove the seeds and stringy pulp from inside the pumpkin and discard.

Step 4 Using a small, sharp knife, work slowly to remove the pulp from inside the pumpkin. Leave a layer of flesh on the skin to form a shell.

Cook's Notes

Time
Preparation takes about 45 minutes, and cooking takes about 20 minutes.

Preparation
If desired, 2 pumpkins may be used, 1 for making the soup and 1 to serve as a tureen. The pumpkin used for cooking must be peeled first.

Variation
Canned pumpkin may also be used for the soup instead of fresh. Soup may be served in a tureen or individual bowls instead of the pumpkin shell, if desired.

SERVES 6-8

GAZPACHO

A recipe you might have sampled
on a Spanish holiday. It's easy and a
perfect starter for summer.

1 medium green pepper, seeded and roughly chopped
8 medium tomatoes, peeled, seeded and roughly chopped
1 large cucumber, peeled and roughly chopped
1 large onion, roughly chopped
90-150g/3-5oz French bread, crusts removed
45ml/3 tbsps red wine vinegar
850ml/1½ pints water
Pinch salt and pepper
1-2 cloves garlic, crushed
45ml/3 tbsps olive oil
10ml/2 tsps tomato purée (optional)

Garnish

1 small onion, diced
½ small cucumber diced, but not peeled
3 tomatoes, peeled, seeded and diced
½ green pepper, seeded and diced

1. Combine all the prepared vegetables in a deep bowl and add the bread, breaking it into small pieces by hand. Mix together thoroughly.

2. Add the vinegar, water, salt, pepper and garlic.

3. Pour the mixture, a third at a time, into a blender or food processor and purée for about 1 minute, or until the soup is smooth.

4. Pour the purée into a clean bowl and gradually beat in the olive oil using a whisk.

5. Cover the bowl tightly and refrigerate for at least 2 hours, or until thoroughly chilled. Before serving, whisk the soup to make sure all the ingredients are blended and then pour into a large chilled soup tureen or into chilled individual soup bowls. Serve all the garnishes in separate bowls to be added to the soup if desired.

Step 2 Add the liquid, seasoning and garlic and stir the mixture well.

Step 4 After puréeing the soup, pour back into a bowl and whisk in the olive oil by hand.

Cook's Notes

Time
Preparation takes about 20 minutes and the soup must chill for at least 2 hours.

Preparation
Gazpacho may be prepared a day in advance and kept overnight in the refrigerator. To quickly chill the soup, omit 280ml/½ pint water from the recipe and use crushed ice instead. Leave refrigerated for 30 minutes, stirring frequently to melt the ice.

Variation
Use only enough garlic to suit your own taste, or omit if desired. Vary the garnishing ingredients by using croûtons, chopped spring onions, or red onions, red or yellow peppers.

SERVES 4

STUFFED EGGS

An inexpensive starter, these can also be a snack
or canapé. The filling is delicious cold, too,
so they are perfect for summer parties and picnics.

4 hard-boiled eggs
225g/8oz cooked ham, minced
60g/4 tbsps grated mild cheese
60g/4 tbsps sour cream
10ml/2 tsps mustard
Pinch salt and pepper
10ml/2 tsps chopped fresh dill or chives
Dry breadcrumbs
Melted butter

1. Using a pin or egg pricker, make a small hole in the larger end of each egg.

2. Lower the eggs gently into boiling water.

3. As the eggs come back to the boil, roll them around with the bowl of a spoon for about 2-3 minutes. This will help set yolk in the middle of the whites. Allow the eggs to cook 9-10 minutes after the water re-boils.

4. Drain and place the eggs under cold running water. Allow to cool completely and leave in the cold water until ready to peel.

5. Peel the eggs, cut them in half lengthways and remove the yolks. Combine yolks and all the remaining ingredients except the breadcrumbs and melted butter and mix well.

6. Pipe or spoon the mixture into each egg white and mound the top, smooth with a small knife. Sprinkle on the breadcrumbs, covering the filling and the edge of the whites completely. Place the eggs in a heatproof dish and drizzle with melted butter. Place under a preheated grill for about 3 minutes, or until crisp and golden brown on top.

Step 1 Using an egg pricker for making a small hole with a pin in the large end of the egg will help prevent the shell from cracking.

Step 3 Use the bowl of the spoon to roll the eggs around in the boiling water to set the yolk.

Step 6 Pipe or spoon the mixture onto each egg white and mound the top.

Cook's Notes

 **Cook's Tip**
Keeping hard-boiled eggs in water until ready to use helps prevent a grey ring from forming around the yolk.

 Time
Preparation takes about 20 minutes, cooking takes about 9-10 minutes for the eggs to boil and 3 minutes for grilling.

 Watchpoint
Do not grill the eggs too long. Overheating will toughen the whites.

SERVES 4

CREAMY CRAB SOUP

Serve this as an elegant starter
for special dinner parties.

1 large crab, cooked
45ml/3 tbsps butter or margarine
1 onion, very finely chopped
30g/2 tbsps flour
1150ml/2 pints milk
90ml/6 tbsps sherry
Pinch salt, white pepper and ground mace
140ml/¼ pint double cream, whipped
Red caviar or chopped chives

1. To dress the crab, take off all the legs and the large claws. Crack the large claws and legs and extract the meat.

2. Turn the crab shell over and press up with thumbs to push out the underbody. Cut this piece in quarters and use a skewer to pick out the meat. Discard the stomach sac and the lungs (dead man's fingers). Set the white meat aside with the claw meat.

3. Using a teaspoon, scrape out the brown meat from inside the shell and reserve it. If the roe is present reserve that, too.

4. Melt the butter or margarine in a medium saucepan and soften the onion for about 3 minutes. Do not allow to brown.

5. Stir in the flour and milk. Bring to the boil and then immediately turn down the heat to simmer. Add the brown meat from the crab and cook gently for about 20 minutes.

6. Add the sherry, salt, pepper, mace, white crab meat and roe. Cook a further 5 minutes.

7. Top each serving with a spoonful of whipped cream and red caviar or chopped chives.

Step 1 Remove the legs and large claws of the crab. Use a rolling pin or meat mallet to crack the large claws and legs to extract the meat.

Step 2 Turn the crab shell over and push out the underbody. Discard stomach sac and lungs.

Step 3 Using a teaspoon, scrape out the brown meat from inside the shell.

Cook's Notes

 Time
Preparation takes about 35-40 minutes and cooking takes about 25 minutes.

 Variation
Frozen crab meat may be substituted. Use about 4-6oz of white crab meat and omit the addition of the brown body meat. Do not use a dressed crab as the brown meat will often have breadcrumbs added to it.

SERVES 4

PEANUT BUTTER SOUP

A velvety rich soup that is easily made from
ordinary store cupboard ingredients. It may sound
strange, but it's really delicious!

60g/4 tbsps butter or margarine
30g/2 tbsps flour
225g/8oz creamy peanut butter
1.25ml/¼ tsp celery seed
700ml/1¼ pints chicken stock
120ml/4 fl oz dry sherry
60g/2oz coarsely chopped peanuts

Step 4 Add the
sherry to the soup
before serving.

Step 2 Once the
peanut butter and
celery seed are
added, gradually
pour in the stock,
stirring or whisking
constantly.

1. Melt the butter or margarine in a medium saucepan.
Remove from the heat and stir in the flour.

2. Add the peanut butter and celery seed. Gradually pour
on the stock, stirring constantly.

3. Return the pan to the heat and simmer gently for about
15 minutes. Do not allow to boil rapidly.

4. Stir in the sherry and ladle into a tureen or individual
bowls. Sprinkle with the chopped peanuts.

Cook's Notes

Time
Preparation takes about 15
minutes and cooking takes
about 15 minutes.

Variation
For a crunchier texture, add 2
sticks of finely diced celery to
the butter or margarine and cook until
slightly softened before adding the
flour.

Preparation
The soup is slightly difficult to
reheat, so it is best prepared
just before serving.

SERVES 2-4

BUTTERED PRAWNS

This make a rich starter or an
elegant main course, yet it's
surprisingly easy.

900g/2lbs cooked prawns
60g/2oz butter, softened
Pinch salt, white pepper and cayenne
1 clove garlic, crushed
90g/6 tbsps fine dry breadcrumbs
30g/2 tbsps chopped parsley
60ml/4 tbsps sherry
Lemon wedges or slices

Step 2 Pull off the tail shell and carefully remove the very end.

Step 1 Remove the heads and legs from the prawns first. Remove any roe at this time.

Step 6 Spread the mixture to completely cover the prawns.

1. To prepare the prawns, remove the heads and legs first.

2. Peel off the shells, carefully removing the tail shells.

3. Remove the black vein running down the length of the rounded side with a cocktail stick. If desired, peeled prawns may be used instead.

4. Arrange prawns in a shallow casserole or individual dishes.

5. Combine the remaining ingredients, except the lemon garnish, mixing well.

6. Spread the mixture to completely cover the prawns and place in a pre-heated 190°C/375°F Gas Mark 5 oven for about 20 minutes, or until the butter melts and the crumbs become crisp. Garnish with lemon wedges or slices.

Cook's Notes

🕐 **Time**
Preparation takes about 35-40 minutes and cooking takes about 20 minutes.

£ **Buying Guide**
Freshly cooked prawns are available from most fishmongers. Substitute frozen prawns, if necessary.

SERVES 4

AVOCADO SOUP

Because this smooth, velvety
soup is served cold, it makes
an easy summer meal.

2 large ripe avocados
430ml/¾ pint natural yogurt
570ml/1 pint chicken or vegetable stock
½ clove garlic, minced
Juice of 1 lemon
10ml/2 tsps chopped fresh oregano
Salt and white pepper
Chopped parsley to garnish

Step 1 Tap the stone with a knife and twist to remove it.

Step 1 Cut the avocados in half and twist to separate.

Step 2 Place the avocado cut side down on a worktop, score the skin and pull it backwards to remove.

1. Cut the avocados in half lengthways and twist to separate. Tap the stone sharply with a knife and twist to remove.

2. Place the avocado halves cut side down on a flat surface. Score the skin with a sharp knife and then peel the strips of skin backwards to remove them.

3. Cut the avocado into pieces and place in a food processor. Reserve 60ml/4 tbsps yogurt and add the remaining yogurt and other ingredients, except the parsley, to the avocado. Process until smooth and chill thoroughly.

4. Pour the soup into bowls or a tureen and garnish with reserved yogurt. Sprinkle with parsley and serve chilled.

Cook's Notes

Time
Preparation takes about 20-25 minutes. The soup should chill for about 2 hours in the refrigerator before serving.

Cook's Tip
The lemon juice, plus the slight acidity of the yogurt, will keep the avocado from turning brown. However, serve the soup on the same day it is prepared.

Preparation
Check the avocado skins and be sure to scrape off any flesh that remains attached to them before processing the ingredients.

SERVES 4

FRESH CREAMED MUSHROOMS

A versatile recipe that's good as
a starter, a side dish or a sauce.

450g/1lb even-sized button mushrooms
15ml/1 tbsp lemon juice
30g/2 tbsps butter or margarine
15g/1 tbsp flour
Salt and white pepper
1.25ml/¼ tsp freshly grated nutmeg
1 small bay leaf
1 blade mace
280ml/½ pint double cream
15ml/1 tbsp dry sherry (optional)

Step 2 Cook the flour gently in the butter for about 1 minute.

Step 1 Trim the mushroom stems level with the caps. Do not use the stems for this recipe.

Step 3 Test with a sharp knife to see if the mushrooms are tender.

1. Wash the mushrooms quickly and dry them well. Trim the stems level with the caps. Leave whole if small, halve or quarter if large. Toss with the lemon juice and set aside. Mushroom stalks can be chopped and added to soups or other sauces.

2. In a medium saucepan, melt the butter or margarine and stir in the flour. Cook, stirring gently, for about 1 minute. Remove from the heat, add the nutmeg, salt, pepper, bay leaf and mace and gradually stir in the cream.

3. Return the pan to the heat and bring to the boil, stirring constantly. Allow to boil for about 1 minute, or until thickened. Reduce the heat and add the mushrooms. Simmer gently, covered, for about 5 minutes, or until the mushrooms are tender. Add the sherry, if using, during the last few minutes of cooking. Remove bay leaf and blade mace. Sprinkle with additional grated nutmeg before serving.

Cook's Notes

Cook's Tip
If the mushrooms are clean, do not wash them. If washing is necessary, rinse them very quickly and pat dry quickly. Mushrooms absorb water easily.

Time
Preparation takes about 20 minutes, and cooking takes about 7 minutes.

Variation
The recipe may be used as a sauce for chicken or ham as well.

Serving Ideas
Serve on hot toast or in individual ramekin dishes or scallop shells, accompanied with hot buttered toast or melba toast. Serves 4 as a starter.

SERVES 8-10

PEA SOUP WITH MINT

This is a summery version of a hearty winter staple.
Green peas and mint add a freshness and a light,
delicate taste to dried split peas.

180g/6oz dried split peas
560g/1¼lbs frozen peas
90g/3oz fresh mint leaves
120g/4oz butter or margarine, melted
Pinch salt and pepper
Sprigs of fresh mint to garnish

Step 3 Cook the frozen peas in the reserved split pea liquid along with the chopped mint.

Step 1 Cook the split peas in water until very soft. Test by mashing some against the side of the pan.

Step 4 Purée the split peas and stir them back into the soup, mixing well.

1. Place the split peas with about 1.7 litres/3 pints water in a heavy saucepan. Cover, bring to the boil and cook until very tender, about 40 minutes.

2. Strain the peas and reserve the liquid.

3. Pour the liquid back into the saucepan and add the frozen peas. Chop the mint leaves, reserving some for garnish, and add to the peas. Bring to the boil in a covered saucepan.

4. Meanwhile, add the melted butter to the dried peas and push through a strainer or work in a food processor to form a smooth purée. Add the puree to the green peas, mixing well. Add salt and pepper to taste.

5. Pour the hot soup into a tureen and garnish with sprigs or leaves of mint. Serve immediately.

Cook's Notes

 Time
Preparation takes about 30 minutes, cooking takes 45-50 minutes.

 Variation
Other fresh herbs, such as marjoram, chervil or thyme may be substituted for the mint.

£ **Buying Guide**
Dried split peas are readily available in supermarkets and health food stores.

SERVES 6-8

CHICKEN NUGGETS

Delicious as a first course or a cocktail
snack, these can be made ahead, then
coated and fried at the last minute.

450g/1lb cooked chicken, minced
4 slices white bread, crusts removed and made into
    crumbs
15g/1 tbsp butter or margarine
15g/1 tbsp flour
140ml/¼ pint milk
1/2 red or green chilli, seeded and finely chopped
1 spring onion, finely chopped
15ml/1 tbsp chopped parsley
Salt
Flour
2 eggs, beaten
Dry breadcrumbs
Oil for frying

1. Combine the chicken with the fresh breadcrumbs and
set aside.

2. Melt the butter and add the flour off the heat. Stir in the
milk and return to moderate heat. Bring to the boil, stirring
constantly.

3. Stir the white sauce into the chicken and breadcrumbs, adding the chilli, onion and parsley. Season with
salt to taste, cover and allow to cool completely.

4. Shape the cold mixture into 2.5cm/1 inch balls with
floured hands.

5. Coat with beaten eggs using a fork to turn balls in the
mixture or use a pastry brush to coat with egg.

Step 4 Flour
hands well and
shape cold crab
mixture into balls.

Step 5 Brush on
beaten egg or dip
into egg to coat.

6. Coat with the dry breadcrumbs.

7. Fry in oil in a deep sauté pan, saucepan or deep-fat fryer
at 180°C/350°F until golden brown and crisp, about 3
minutes per batch of 6. Turn occasionally while frying.

8. Drain on paper towels and sprinkle lightly with salt.

Cook's Notes

Time
Preparation takes about 40-50
minutes, including time for the
mixture to cool. A batch of 6 balls takes
about 3 minutes to cook.

Variation
Use finely chopped prawns
instead of chicken. Omit chilli
if desired, or use a quarter red or green
pepper.

£ Economy
Cooked whitefish such as
haddock or whiting can be
substituted.

SERVES 6-8

CREAMY SHELLFISH SOUP

Buy fresh or frozen cockles for this
filling recipe. The variety packed in brine
or vinegar will spoil the soup's taste.

90g/3oz rindless streaky bacon, diced
2 medium onions, finely diced
15ml/1 tbsp flour
6 medium potatoes, peeled and cubed
Salt and pepper
1150ml/2 pints milk
140ml/¼pint fish stock
280ml/½ pint single cream
450g/1lb fresh or frozen cockles
Chopped parsley (optional)

Step 2 Cook the onion in the bacon fat until soft and transluscent.

Step 1 Cook the bacon slowly until the fat renders.

Step 3 Cook the onion in the bacon fat until soft and translucent.

1. Place the diced bacon in a large, deep saucepan and cook slowly until the fat is rendered. Turn up the heat and brown the bacon. Remove it to paper towel to drain.

2. Add the onions to the bacon fat in the pan and cook slowly to soften. Stir in the flour and add the potatoes, salt, pepper, milk and fish stock.

3. Cover and bring to the boil and cook for about 10 minutes, or until the potatoes are nearly tender. Add cockles to the soup along with the cream and diced bacon. Cook a further 10 minutes, or until the potatoes and cockles are tender. Add the chopped parsley, if desired, and serve immediately.

Cook's Notes

Time
Preparation takes about 30 minutes and cooking takes about
20 minutes.

Cook's Tip
You can make your own fish stock or dissolve half of a fish stock cube in water.

Buying Guide
Substitute either fresh, frozen or canned mussels, if preferred.

SERVES 8-10

RED BEAN AND RED PEPPER SOUP

A nutritious and warming soup
that's very economical.

450g/1lb dried red kidney beans
Water to cover
2 onions, coarsely chopped
3 sticks celery, coarsely chopped
2 bay leaves
Salt and pepper
3 large red peppers, seeded and finely chopped
2.5 litres/5 pints chicken stock
Lemon wedges and 4 chopped hard-boiled eggs to
  garnish

3. Bring to the boil over high heat, stirring occasionally. Reduce the heat and allow to simmer, partially covered, for about 3 hours or until the beans are completely tender.

4. Remove the bay leaves and purée the soup in a food processor or blender.

5. Serve garnished with the chopped hard-boiled egg. Serve lemon wedges on the side.

Step 1 Soak the beans overnight in enough water to cover, or boil for two minutes and leave to soak for an hour. The beans will swell in size.

Step 2 Combine the beans with the other ingredients in a large stock pot and pour on enough chicken stock to cover.

Step 3 When the beans are soft enough to mash easily, remove bay leaves and purée the soup.

1. Soak the beans in the water overnight. Alternatively, bring them to the boil and boil rapidly for 2 minutes. Leave to stand for 1 hour.

2. Drain off the liquid and add the onions, celery, bay leaves, salt and pepper, red peppers and stock.

Cook's Notes

Time
Preparation takes about 25 minutes, with overnight soaking for the beans. Cooking takes about 3 hours.

Watchpoint
It is dangerous to eat dried pulses that are not thoroughly cooked. Make sure the beans are very soft before puréeing.

Freezing
The soup may be prepared and puréed in advance and frozen for up to 3 months. Freeze in small containers so that the soup will defrost faster. Defrost at room temperature, breaking the mixture up with a fork as the soup defrosts.

SERVES 4-6

AVOCADO MOULDS

A cooling treat in summer or a
perfect do-ahead dish anytime.

Juice of 1 small lemon
25g/1½ tbsps gelatine
2 ripe avocados
90g/3oz cream cheese or low fat soft cheese
140ml/¼ pint sour cream or natural yogurt
30ml/2 tbsps mayonnaise
3 oranges, peeled and segmented
Flat Italian parsley or coriander to garnish

Step 6 Pour the avocado mixture into oiled ramekin dishes with a piece of greaseproof paper in the bottom.

1. Reserve about 10ml/2 tsps of the lemon juice. Pour the rest into a small dish, sprinkle the gelatine on top and allow to stand until spongy.

2. Cut the avocados in half and twist to separate. Reserve half of one avocado with the stone attached and brush the cut surface with lemon juice, wrap in cling film and keep in the refrigerator.

3. Remove the stone from the other half and scrape the pulp from the three halves into a food processor.

4. Add the cheese, sour cream or yogurt and mayonnaise and process until smooth.

5. Melt the gelatine and add it to the avocado mixture with the machine running.

6. Place a small disc of greaseproof paper in ramekin dishes, oil the sides of the dishes and the paper and pour in the mixture. Tap the dishes lightly on a flat surface to smooth the top and eliminate any air bubbles, cover with cling film and chill until set.

7. Loosen the set mixture carefully from the sides of the dishes and invert each onto a serving plate to unmould. Peel and slice the remaining avocado half and use to decorate the plate along with the orange segments. Place parsley or coriander leaves on top of each avocado mould to serve.

Step 7 Make sure the mixture pulls away completely from the sides of the dishes before inverting and shaking to unmould.

Cook's Notes

Time
Preparation takes about 25 minutes. The salads will take about 2 hours to set completely.

Cook's Tip
Adding lemon juice to the mixture and brushing the avocado slices with lemon juice will help to keep them from turning brown. The salad will discolour slightly even with the addition of lemon juice if kept in the refrigerator more than one day.

Preparation
The avocado salad may be kept in the refrigerator overnight and turned out the next day. Do not keep longer than a day in the refrigerator.

SERVES 6

PRAWN SOUP

A hearty soup that makes a meal
accompanied by some crusty bread.

45g/3 tbsps butter or margarine
1 onion, finely chopped
1 red pepper, seeded and finely chopped
2 sticks celery, finely chopped
1 clove garlic, minced
Pinch dry mustard
10ml/2 tsps paprika
45g/3 tbsps flour
1150ml/2 pints fish stock
1 sprig thyme and bay leaf
225g/8oz raw, peeled prawns
Salt and pepper
Snipped chives

Step 2 Cook the mustard, cayenne, paprika and flour briefly until the mixture darkens in colour.

1. Melt the butter or margarine and add the onion, pepper, celery and garlic. Cook gently to soften.

2. Stir in the mustard, paprika and flour. Cook about 3 minutes over gentle heat, stirring occasionally.

3. Pour on the stock gradually, stirring until well blended. Add the thyme and bay leaf and bring to the boil. Reduce the heat and simmer about 5 minutes or until thickened, stirring occasionally.

4. Add the prawns and cook until pink and curled, about 5 minutes. Season with salt and pepper to taste and top with snipped chives before serving.

Step 3 Pour on the stock gradually and stir or whisk until well blended.

Step 4 Use kitchen scissors to snip the chives finely over the top of the soup before serving.

Cook's Notes

Time
Preparation takes about 20 minutes and cooking takes about 8-10 minutes.

Variation
If using peeled, cooked prawns add just before serving and heat through for about 2 minutes only.

Cook's Tip
Cook spices such as paprika briefly before adding any liquid to develop their flavour and eliminate harsh taste.

SERVES 8

STUFFED PEPPERS

Organization is the key to preparing these
stuffed peppers. Fried inside their golden
batter coating, they're puffy and light.

Full quantity Tomato Sauce (see recipe for Tomato Beef
    Stir-fry)
8 small green peppers
1 clove garlic, crushed
2.5ml/½ tsp rubbed sage
225g/8oz cream cheese
225g/8oz grated mild cheese
Salt
Flour for dredging
Oil for deep frying
8 eggs, separated
90g/6 tbsps plain flour
Pinch salt
Finely chopped spring onions

1. Blanch the whole peppers in boiling water for about
10-15 minutes, or until just tender. Rinse them in cold water
and pat them dry.

2. Carefully cut around the stems to make a top, remove
and set aside. Scoop out the seeds and cores, leaving the
peppers whole.

3. Mix together the garlic, sage, cheeses and salt to taste.
Fill the peppers using a small teaspoon and replace the
tops, sticking them into the filling.

4. Dredge the peppers with flour and heat the oil in a deep
fat fryer to 180°C/375°F.

5. Beat the egg yolks and flour in a mixing bowl until the
mixture forms a ribbon trail when the beaters are lifted.

6. Beat the whites with a pinch of salt until stiff but not dry.
Fold into the egg yolk mixture.

7. Shape 30ml/2 tbsps of batter into an oval and drop into
the oil. Immediately slide a metal draining spoon under the
batter to hold it in place. Place on a filled pepper. Cover the
tops of the peppers with more batter and then spoon over
hot oil to seal. Fry until the batter is brown on all sides,
turning the peppers over carefully.

8. Drain on paper towels and keep them warm on a rack in
a moderate oven while frying the remaining peppers.

9. Sprinkle with onions and serve with Tomato Sauce.

Step 2 Carefully
cut around the
stems of each
blanched pepper
to make a top.

Step 7 Cover the
tops of the peppers
with more batter
and spoon over oil
to seal.

Cook's Notes

 Time
Preparation takes about 40
minutes and cooking takes
about 3 minutes per pepper. Red
Sauce will take approximately 15
minutes to cook.

Cook's Tip
Sprinkling savoury foods
lightly with salt helps to draw
out any excess oil. For fried sweet
foods, substitute sugar.

 Serving Ideas
Peppers may be served as a
main course with a salad and
rice. These also make a good starter.

2

EGG
&
CHEESE
DISHES

pages 54-65

SERVES 2

BACON, PEPPER AND TOMATO OMELETTE

4 rashers back bacon, diced
Half a small onion, chopped
Half a small green pepper, seeded and chopped
1 tomato, seeded and diced
3 eggs, beaten
Salt and pepper
15g/1 tbsp grated cheese
Parsley to garnish

Step 3 Pour in the egg, tomato and cheese mixture and stir once or twice to mix thoroughly.

Step 2 Cook the onion, green pepper and bacon until the vegetables are soft and the bacon is crisp.

Step 4 Place under a pre-heated grill to cook the top until golden brown and slightly puffy.

1. Heat a medium-size frying pan or omelette pan. Add the bacon and sauté slowly until the fat is rendered.

2. Turn up the heat and cook until the bacon begins to brown and crisp. Add the onion and green pepper and cook to soften and finish off the bacon.

3. Mix the tomato with the eggs, salt, pepper and cheese. Pour into the pan and stir once or twice with a

fork to mix all the ingredients. Cook until lightly browned on the underside.

4. Place under a pre-heated grill and cook the top quickly until brown and slightly puffy.

5. Garnish with parsley, cut into wedges and serve immediately.

Cook's Notes

Time
Preparation takes about 25 minutes and cooking takes about 10-15 minutes.

Cook's Tip
15ml/1 tbsp of water added to the eggs before beating will produce a lighter, fluffier omelette.

Serving Ideas
Serve as a light main course for supper or lunch. As a starter, this will serve 4 people.

SERVES 4

EGGS FLORENTINE

Recipes called "Florentine" have a base
of spinach. The versatile sauce can be
used on vegetables or fish, as well.

675g/1½lbs fresh spinach
25g/1½ tbsps butter or margarine
15g/1 tbsp flour
280ml/½ pint milk
Salt, pepper and nutmeg
4 canned artichoke hearts, quartered
4 eggs

Hollandaise Sauce

3 egg yolks
180g/6oz unsalted butter
15ml/1 tbsp lemon juice
Pinch salt and pepper
1 large piece canned pimento, drained and cut into thin
   strips

1. Strip the spinach leaves from the stalks and wash the leaves well. Place the leaves in a large saucepan and add a pinch of salt. Cover the pan and cook the spinach over moderate heat in only the water that clings to the leaves. When the spinach is just wilted, take off the heat and drain well. Chop roughly and set aside.

2. Melt the butter or margarine in a medium-sized saucepan and stir in the flour. Gradually add the milk, whisking constantly, and place the sauce over low heat. Whisk the sauce as it comes to the boil and allow it to boil rapidly for about one minute to thicken. Stir in the spinach and season the sauce with salt, pepper and nutmeg. Add the artichoke hearts and set the sauce aside.

3. Fill a large sauté pan with water and bring to the boil. Turn down the heat and, when the water is just barely simmering, break an egg into a cup or onto a saucer.

Gently lower the egg into the water to poach. Repeat with the remaining eggs. Poach over gentle heat, never allowing the water to boil. Alternatively, cook in a special poaching pan. Cook until the whites have set but the yolks are still soft. Remove the eggs from the pan with a draining spoon and place in cold water until ready to use.

4. Place the egg yolks in a food processor or blender with the lemon juice and seasoning. Process once or twice to mix. Place the butter in a small saucepan and melt over gentle heat. Turn up the heat and when the butter is bubbling, take off the heat. With the machine running, gradually pour the butter onto the eggs in a very thin but steady stream.

5. To assemble the dish, reheat the spinach sauce and place an equal amount of it on each plate. Make a well in centre. Place the eggs back into hot water briefly to reheat, and drain well. Place an egg in the hollow of the spinach sauce on each plate. Spoon over some of the Hollandaise sauce to coat each egg completely. Make a cross with two strips of pimento on top of each egg and serve immediately.

Step 5 To reheat eggs, place briefly in hot water, remove with a draining spoon and hold over a towel to drain and dry completely.

Cook's Notes

Time
Preparation takes about 45 minutes and cooking takes about 5 minutes for the spinach, 5-10 minutes for the sauce and about 5-6 minutes for the eggs.

Cook's Tip
If eggs should curdle when making a Hollandaise sauce, 15ml/1 tbsp iced water worked into the sauce quickly can sometimes bring it together again.

Variation
Artichoke hearts may be omitted and mushrooms used instead. Omit the pimento cross on top and sprinkle lightly with paprika before serving.

SERVES 4

HOLLANDAISE AND MUSHROOM EGGS

Organization it the key to preparing this rich egg dish.

Full quantity Hollandaise sauce from the recipe for Eggs
   Florentine
4 eggs
4 slices smoked streaky bacon
1 beefsteak tomato
4 slices bread
Oil for frying

Mushroom Sauce

45ml/3 tbsps oil
½ small onion, finely chopped
25g/1½ tbsps flour
1 clove garlic
6 mushrooms, finely chopped
180ml/6 fl oz brown stock
Salt and pepper

1. Heat the oil for the Mushroom sauce. Add the onion and cook until softened. Add the flour and cook slowly stirring frequently, until golden brown. Add the garlic and mushrooms and pour on the stock, stirring to blend well, and bring the sauce to the boil. Lower the heat and simmer for about 15-20 minutes, stirring occasionally. Season to taste.

2. Prepare the Hollandaise sauce and poach the eggs according to the recipe for Eggs Florentine.

3. Fry the bacon in a small amount of oil, or grill until crisp. Drain, crumble and set aside.

4. Cut the bread with a pastry cutter into 7.5cm/3 inch diameter rounds. Fry in enough oil to just cover until golden brown and crisp. Drain on paper towels and place on a serving plate. Spoon some of the Mushroom sauce on top and keep warm in the oven.

5. Slice the tomatoes thickly and place one slice on top of the sauce on each fried bread round and continue to keep warm.

6. Reheat the eggs and drain well. Place one egg on top of each tomato slice. Spoon over some of the Hollandaise sauce and sprinkle with the bacon to serve.

Step 1 Add the flour and cook slowly until a golden brown, stirring frequently.

Step 4 To fry the bread, cut into circles and place in the oil, holding the bread under the oil with a fish slice to brown both sides quickly. Drain on paper towels.

Cook's Notes

Time
Preparation takes about 45 minutes and cooking takes about 15 minutes for the Mushroom sauce and about 30 minutes total time.

Cook's Tip
Hollandaise sauce may be reheated by pouring the sauce into a bowl and placing the bowl in a pan of hot water. Stir the sauce frequently until evenly heated through. Never reheat over direct heat.

Preparation
The Mushroom sauce may be prepared several days in advance and kept in the refrigerator. Reheat gently until boiling.

SERVES 6

TOMATO AND CHEESE LASAGNE

With its layers of red, green and white it looks as delicious
as it tastes so you won't even miss the meat!

9 sheets spinach lasagne pasta

Tomato Sauce

45ml/3 tbsps olive oil
2 cloves garlic, crushed
900g/2lbs fresh tomatoes, peeled, or canned tomatoes,
  drained
2 tbsps chopped fresh basil, six whole leaves reserved
Salt and pepper
Pinch sugar

Cheese Filling

450g/1lb ricotta cheese or cottage cheese, drained well
60g/4 tbsps unsalted butter
225g/8oz Mozzarella cheese, grated
Salt and pepper
Pinch nutmeg

1. Cook the pasta for 8 minutes in boiling salted water with
15ml/1 tbsp oil. Drain and rinse under hot water and place
in a single layer on a damp cloth. Cover with another damp
cloth and set aside.

2. To prepare the sauce, cook the garlic in remaining oil for
about 1 minute in a large saucepan. When pale brown, add
the tomatoes, basil, salt, pepper and sugar. If using fresh
tomatoes, drop into boiling water for 6-8 seconds. Transfer
to cold water and leave to cool completely. This will make
the peels easier to remove.

3. Lower the heat under the saucepan and simmer the
sauce for 35 minutes. Add more seasoning or sugar to
taste.

4. Beat the ricotta or cottage cheese and butter together
until creamy and stir into the remaining ingredients.

5. To assemble the lasagne, oil a rectangular baking dish
and place 3 sheets of lasagne on the base. Cover with one
third of the sauce and carefully spread on a layer of cheese.
Place another 3 layers of pasta over the cheese and cover
with another third of the sauce. Add the remaining cheese
filling and cover with the remaining pasta. Spoon the
remaining sauce on top.

6. Cover with foil and bake for 20 minutes at 190°C/375°F/
Gas Mark 5. Uncover and cook for 10 minutes longer.
Garnish with the reserved leaves and leave to stand 10-15
minutes before serving.

Step 5 Place
pasta on the base
of an oiled baking
dish. Spread
tomato sauce
over.

Step 5 Carefully
spread the
softened cheese
mixture on top of
the tomato sauce.

Cook's Notes

Cook's Tip
Lasagne can be assembled
the day before and
refrigerated. Allow 5-10 minutes more
cooking time in the oven if not at room
temperature.

Time
Preparation takes about 25
minutes, cooking takes about
1-1¼ hours.

Variations
Use plain pasta instead, if
desired. If using pre-cooked
lasagne pasta, follow the baking times
in the package directions.

SERVES 4

POACHED EGGS IN VEGETABLE NESTS

4 heads chicory
1 large red pepper, roasted (see Chicken with Red
   . Peppers)
1 large or 2 small courgettes, cut into matchstick pieces
1 small celeriac, cut into matchstick pieces
2-3 spring onions, shredded
1 pepperoni sausage, blanched and cut into thin strips
4 eggs
60g/4 tbsps pine nuts

Dressing

5ml/1 tsp chopped fresh coriander
90ml/6 tbsps oil
30ml/2 tbsps lemon juice
Dash tabasco
Salt and pinch sugar

1. Prepare the roasted pepper and cut it into thin strips. Blanch the pepperoni for about 5 minutes in boiling water. Drain and peel off skin.

2. Separate the leaves of the chicory and slice or leave whole if small.

3. Bring water to the boil and blanch the courgettes and celeriac strips for one minute. Rinse under cold water until completely cool and leave to drain. Combine with the chicory. Add the strips of pepperoni and set aside.

4. Toast the pine nuts in a moderate oven until golden brown, about 5 minutes.

5. Bring at least 5cm/2 inches of water to the boil in a frying or sauté pan. Turn down the heat to simmering. Break an egg onto a saucer or into a cup.

6. Stir the water to make a whirlpool and then carefully pour the egg into the centre, keeping the saucer or cup close to the level of the water. When the water stops swirling

and the white begins to set, gently move the egg over to the side and repeat with each remaining egg. Cook the eggs until the whites are completely set, but the yolks are still soft.

7. Remove the eggs from the water with a draining spoon and place them immediately into a bowl of cold water.

8. Mix the dressing ingredients together and pour half over the vegetables and pepperoni. Toss to coat. Arrange the mixture on individual plates in the shape of nests.

9. Remove the eggs from the cold water with the draining spoon and hold them over a towel for a few minutes to drain completely. Place one egg in the middle of each nest. Spoon the remaining dressing over each egg, sprinkle over the pine nuts and garnish the yolk with a coriander leaf.

Step 6 To poach the eggs, make a whirlpool in the water and carefully pour the egg into the centre.

Step 8 Arrange the vegetable mixture in the shape of a nest on a serving plate and carefully spoon an egg into the middle.

Cook's Notes

Time
Preparation takes about 45 minutes and cooking takes about 5 minutes for the eggs, 1 minute to blanch the vegetables and 10 minutes to blanch the pepperoni.

Serving Ideas
Double the quantity of the vegetables and pepperoni and serve as a light lunch or supper dish. The salad may also be served as a starter.

SERVES 6

CHEESE AND BACON QUICHE

This savoury flan originated in France
but is now popular everywhere.

Pastry

120g/4oz butter
180g/6oz plain flour, sifted
Pinch salt
1 egg
10ml/2 tsps ice water

Filling

6 strips smoked streaky bacon, cut into large dice
5ml/1 tsp butter or margarine
2 shallots, finely chopped
2 eggs plus 2 egg yolks
280ml/½ pint cream
Salt, pepper and grated nutmeg
45g/3oz grated cheese

Step 2 Use rolling pin to lift pastry into dish.

1. Preheat the oven to 190°C/375°F/Gas Mark 5. To prepare the pastry, sift the flour and salt into a large bowl. Rub in the butter until the mixture looks like fine breadcrumbs – this may also be done in a food processor. Beat the egg lightly and mix into the flour by hand or with the machine. If the dough seems crumbly, add some of the water. Chill well before using. Alternatively use 180g/6oz bought shortcrust pastry.

2. Roll the pastry out to a circle about 5mm/¼ inch thick on a well-floured surface. Roll the pastry over a rolling pin and unroll it onto a 20-22.5cm/8-9 inch flan dish. Gently press the pastry into the bottom and up the sides of the dish, being careful not to stretch it. Trim off the excess pastry by running the rolling pin over the rim of the dish or using a

sharp knife. Prick the bottom of the pastry lightly with a fork.

3. Place a circle of greaseproof paper on top of the pastry and fill with dry beans, or rice. Bake for about 10 minutes, remove the paper and filing. Prick the base again lightly and return to the oven for another 3 minutes or until just beginning to brown. Allow the pastry to cool while preparing filling.

4. Place the bacon in a small frying pan and fry over gentle heat until the fat begins to run. Raise the heat and cook until lightly browned and crisp. Place the bacon on paper towels to drain and add butter to the pan if insufficient fat left. Add chopped shallots and cook until just beginning to colour. Remove to the paper towel to drain with the bacon.

5. Beat the eggs and extra yolks, cream and seasonings together in a large bowl. Scatter the bacon and shallots over the bottom of the pastry case and ladle the custard filling on top of it. Top with cheese.

6. Bake in the top half of the oven for about 25 minutes, or until the custard has puffed and browned and a knife inserted into the centre comes out clean. Allow to cool slightly and then remove from dish, serve directly from the dish.

Cook's Notes

Time
Preparation takes about 25 minutes, plus time for chilling the pastry. Cooking takes about 40 minutes.

Preparation
Baking a pastry case without a filling is called baking blind. By pricking the bottom of the pastry, lining it with paper and filing with rice or beans you help the pastry hold its shape.

Variation
Use basic pastry and custard recipes, but substitute other ingredients such as ham, shellfish or vegetables for the bacon.

3

FISH
— & —
SEAFOOD

SERVES 4

MUSSELS IN WHITE WINE SAUCE

Mussels in season are very economical.
Most fishmongers sell them and so do
supermarkets that have fresh fish counters.

2kg/4½lbs mussels in their shells
Flour or cornmeal
280ml/½ pint dry white wine
1 large onion, finely chopped
2-4 cloves garlic, finely chopped
Salt and coarsely ground black pepper
2 bay leaves
225g/8oz butter, melted
Juice of 1 lemon

1. Scrub the mussels well and remove any barnacles and beards (seaweed strands). Use a stiff brush to scrub the shells, and discard any mussels with broken shells or those that do not close when tapped.

2. Place the mussels in a basin full of cold water with a handful of flour and leave to soak for 30 minutes.

3. Drain the mussels and place them in a large, deep saucepan with the remaining ingredients, except the butter and lemon juice. Cover the pan and bring to the boil.

4. Stir the mussels occasionally while they are cooking to help them cook evenly. Cook about 5-8 minutes, or until the shells open. Discard any mussels that do not open.

5. Spoon the mussels into individual serving bowls and strain the cooking liquid. Pour the liquid into 4 small bowls and serve with the mussels and a bowl of melted butter mixed with lemon juice for each person. Dip the mussels into the broth and the melted butter to eat. Use a mussel shell to scoop out each mussel, or eat with small forks or spoons.

Step 1 Scrub the mussels with a stiff brush to remove barnacles and seaweed beards.

Step 1 To test if the mussels are still alive, tap them on a work surface – the shells should close.

Step 5 Hold a mussel shell between 2 fingers and pinch together to remove mussels from their shells to eat.

Cook's Notes

 Time
Preparation takes about 30 minutes, and cooking takes about 5-8 minutes.

 Cook's Tip
The beards are strands of seaweed that anchor the mussels to the rocks on which they grow. These must be removed before cooking. They can be pulled off quite easily by hand, or scrubbed off with a stiff brush.

 Variation
Use the amount of garlic that suits your own taste or leave out the garlic, if desired. Chopped fresh herbs may be added.

SERVES 4

STUFFED TROUT WITH YOGURT SAUCE

1 boned trout, (about 900g/2lb in boned weight)
225g/8oz ham
Water
1 small green pepper, seeded and finely chopped
2 small onions, finely chopped
1 slice bread, made into crumbs
60ml/4 tbsps lemon juice
Lemon juice
140ml/¼ pint natural yogurt
5ml/1 tsp garlic powder
10ml/2 tsps chopped coriander
Salt and pepper

1. Have the fishmonger bone the trout, leaving the head and tail on the fish.

2. Combine ham with the green pepper, onion, breadcrumbs and lemon juice.

3. Sprinkle the fish cavity with salt and pepper.

4. Stuff the fish with the sausage mixture and place on lightly-oiled foil. Seal the ends to form a parcel and bake in a pre-heated 180°C/350°F/Gas Mark 4 oven for about 20-30 minutes, or until the fish feels firm and the flesh looks opaque.

5. Combine the yogurt, garlic powder, coriander and seasonings to taste.

6. Remove the fish from the foil and transfer to a serving plate. Spoon some of the sauce over the fish and serve the rest separately.

Step 3 Sprinkle the fish cavity with lemon juice.

Step 4 When the stuffing ingredients are well mixed, spoon into the fish on one half and press the other half down lightly to spread the stuffing evenly.

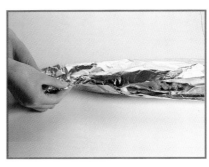

Step 4 Seal the foil loosely around the fish.

Cook's Notes

Time
Preparation takes about 25 minutes and cooking takes about 10 minutes for pre-cooking the sausage and 25 minutes for cooking the fish.

Variation
Other whole fish such as sea bass or grey mullet may be used with the stuffing, however, the stuffing doesn't compliment salmon.

SERVES 4

CRUNCHY COD

Cod provides the perfect base for a
crunchy, slightly spicy topping.

4 even-sized cod fillets
Salt and pepper
90g/6 tbsps butter, melted
90g/3oz dry breadcrumbs
5ml/1 tsp dry mustard
5ml/1 tsp minced onion
Dash Worcester sauce and tabasco
30ml/2 tbsps lemon juice
15ml/1 tbsp finely chopped parsley

Step 3 Press the crumbs gently to pack them into place using a spoon or your hand.

Step 1 Season the fish lightly with salt and pepper and brush with some of the melted butter. Grill to pre-cook but do not brown.

1. Season the fish fillets with salt and pepper and place them on a grill tray. Brush with butter and grill for about 5 minutes.

2. Combine remaining butter with breadcrumbs, mustard, onion salt, Worcester sauce, tabasco, lemon juice and parsley.

3. Spoon the mixture carefully on top of each fish fillet, covering it completely. Press down lightly to pack the crumbs into place. Grill for a further 5-7 minutes, or until the top is lightly browned and the fish flakes.

Cook's Notes

Time
Preparation takes about 15 minutes and cooking takes about 12 minutes.

Preparation
If desired, the fish may also be baked in the oven. Cover the fish with foil foe first 5 minutes of baking time, uncover and top with the breadcrumb mixture. Bake for a further 10-12 minutes at 180°C/350°F/Gas Mark 4.

Variation
The breadcrumb topping may be used on other fish such as haddock, halibut or sole.

SERVES 4

SCAMPI AURORA

The name comes from the rosy pink
sauce. For the occasional extravagant
dinner, this dish is perfect!

90g/6 tbsps butter or margarine
1 small onion, chopped
450g/1lb scampi
90g/6 tbsps flour
280ml/½ pint water or fish stock
15ml/1 tbsp tomato purée
30ml/2 tbsps chopped parsley
10ml/2 tsps chopped dill
Salt and pepper
Cooked rice

Step 1 Cook the
onion and scampi
quickly until the
scampi curls up.

1. Melt half the butter or margarine, add the onion and
cook to soften slightly. Add scampi and cook quickly until it
curls. Remove to a plate.

2. Add the flour to the pan and cook slowly until golden
brown, stirring frequently.

3. Pour on the water and stir vigorously to blend. Add
tomato purée and bring to the boil. Add parsley, dill,
and seasoning to taste and return the onions and the
scampi to the sauce. Heat through for 5 minutes and
serve over rice.

Step 3 Add the
water gradually,
stirring vigorously.
The mixture
should be very
thick.

Step 3 Return the
scampi and
onions to the
sauce to heat
through. Juices
from both will thin
down the sauce.

Cook's Notes

Time
Preparation takes about 20
minutes and cooking takes
about 15 minutes.

Watchpoint
Prawns, scampi and other
types of seafood become very
tough if cooked too quickly or over heat
that is too high.

Variation
Scampi are usually available
from fishmongers. If you can't
get them use cooked, peeled prawns.
Add them at the last and heat through
5 minutes.

SERVES 4

SALMON PIES

Use economical canned pink
salmon in a very unusual
and tasty way.

Pastry
225g/8oz plain flour, sifted
Pinch salt
120-180g/4-6oz butter or margarine
Cold water

Filling
1 large can pink salmon
45ml/3 tbsps oil
45g/3 tbsps flour
½ green pepper, seeded and finely diced
2 spring onions, finely chopped
1 stick celery, finely chopped
280ml/½ pint
Salt and pepper

Step 6 Roll the pastry out thinly and use a rolling pin to transfer it to the baking dish.

1. Sift the flour in a bowl with a pinch of salt and rub in the butter or margarine until the mixture resembles the breadcrumbs. Add enough cold water to bring the mixture together. Knead into a ball, wrap well and chill for about 30 minutes before use.

2. Drain salmon and remove any skin. Discard small bones.

3. Heat the oil in a small saucepan for the filling and add the flour. Cook slowly, stirring constantly until the flour turns a rich dark brown.

4. Add the remaining filling ingredients, stirring constantly while adding the milk. Bring to the boil, reduce the heat and cook for about 5 minutes. Add the salmon to the sauce.

5. Divide the pastry into 4 and roll out each portion on a lightly-floured surface to about 5mm/¼ inch thick.

6. Line individual flan or pie dishes with the pastry, pushing it carefully onto the base and down the sides, taking care not to stretch it. Trim off excess pastry and reserve.

7. Place a sheet of greaseproof paper or foil on the pastry and pour on rice, pasta or baking beans to come halfway up the sides. Bake the pastry blind for about 10 minutes in a pre-heated 200°C/400°F/Gas Mark 6 oven.

8. Remove the paper and beans and bake for an additional 5 minutes to cook the base.

9. Spoon in the filling and roll out any trimmings to make a lattice pattern on top. Bake a further 10 minutes to brown the lattice and heat the filling. Cool slightly before serving.

Cook's Notes

Time
Preparation takes about 30 minutes and cooking takes about 10 minutes for the filling and 25 minutes to finish the dish.

Cook's Tip
Baking the pastry blind helps it to crisp on the base and brown evenly without overcooking the filling.

Serving Ideas
Serve as a light main course with a salad, or make smaller pies to serve as a first course.

SERVES 4

SPICY FRIED FISH

The spice mixture is *very* hot,
so use less if you want.

4 fish fillets, about 225g/8oz each
225g/8oz unsalted butter
15ml/1 tbsp paprika
5ml/1 tsp garlic granules
5ml/1 tsp cayenne pepper
2.5ml/½ tsp ground white pepper
10ml/2 tsps salt
5ml/1 tsp dried thyme

1. Melt the butter and pour about half into each of four ramekin dishes and set aside.

2. Brush each fish fillet liberally with the remaining butter on both sides.

3. Mix together the spices and thyme and sprinkle generously on each side of the fillets, patting it on by hand.

4. Heat a large frying pan and add about 15ml/1 tbsp butter per fish fillet. When the butter is hot, add the fish, skin side down first.

5. Turn the fish over when the underside is very brown and repeat with the remaining side. Add more butter as necessary during cooking.

6. When the top side of the fish is very dark brown, repeat with the remaining fish fillets, keeping them warm while cooking the rest.

7. Serve the fish immediately with the dishes of butter for dipping.

Step 2 Use a pastry brush to coat the fish well on both sides with the melted butter. Alternatively, spoon the butter over or dip the fish in the butter.

Step 3 Mix the seasoning ingredients together well and press firmly onto both sides of the fish to coat.

Step 5 Cook the underside and topside of the fish until very dark brown.

Cook's Notes

Time
Preparation takes about 20 minutes and cooking takes about 2 minutes per side for each fillet.

Variation
Use whatever varieties of fish fillets or steaks you like but make sure they are approximately 2cm ¾ inch thick.

Preparation
The fish should be very dark brown on the top and the bottom before serving. Leave at least 2 minutes before attempting to turn the fish over.

SERVES 4

TOMATO FISH STEW

Cook any white fish you like
in this tomato sauce. Serve
with rice or potatoes.

Fishbones
1 bay leaf, 1 sprig thyme and 2 parsley stalks
2 slices onion
1 lemon slice
6 black peppercorns
430ml/¾ pint water
90ml/6 tbsps oil
90g/6 tbsps flour
1 large green pepper, seeded and finely chopped
1 onion, finely chopped
1 stick celery, finely chopped
900g/2lbs canned tomatoes
30g/2 tbsps tomato purée
Pinch salt and allspice
90ml/6 tbsps white wine
2 whole plaice, filleted and skinned
30ml/2 tbsps chopped parsley

3. Add the green pepper, onion and celery, and cook until the flour is a rich dark brown and the vegetables have softened.

4. Add stock and the canned tomatoes, tomato purée, salt and allspice. Bring to the boil and then simmer until thick. Add the wine.

5. Cut the fish fillets into 5cm/2 inch pieces and add to the tomato mixture. Cook slowly for about 20 minutes, or until the fish is tender. Gently stir in the parsley, taking care that the fish does not break up. Adjust the seasoning and serve.

Step 4 Simmer the tomato mixture until very thick.

Step 4 Pour the fish stock onto the oil and flour mixture, whisking constantly to form a smooth paste.

Step 5 Cut the fish fillets into 5cm/2 inch pieces and add to the tomato mixture.

1. Place fish bones, herbs, onion, lemon slice, peppercorns and water in a saucepan. Bring to the boil, then simmer 20 minutes and strain.

2. Heat the oil and add the flour. Cook slowly, stirring constantly, until golden brown

Cook's Notes

 Time
Preparation takes about 30 minutes and cooking takes about 20 minutes for the fish stock and 20 minutes to finish the dish.

Preparation
Fish stock can be prepared a day in advance and refrigerated. It can also be frozen.

 Variation
Wine may be replaced with 45ml/3 tbsps lemon juice and 45ml/5 tbsps water.

SERVES 4

STUFFED BAKED TROUT

Three kinds of ground pepper make this
stuffing quite spicy hot. Cut down the
amount a bit, if liked.

Step 1 Trim the
fins, neaten the
tail of the trout and
rinse well. Pat dry.

4 whole trout, about 225g/8oz each
120g/4oz butter or margarine
1 onion, finely chopped
2 sticks celery, finely chopped
1 small red pepper, seeded and finely chopped
4 spring onions, finey chopped
1 clove garlic, crushed
10ml/2 tsps chopped parsley
5ml/1 tsp chopped fresh dill
1.25ml/¼ tsp white pepper
1.25ml/¼ tsp cayenne pepper
1.25ml/¼ tsp black pepper
Pinch salt
120g/4oz dry breadcrumbs
2 small eggs, lightly beaten

1. Wash the trout well inside and pat dry.

2. Melt half the butter or margarine in a medium saucepan. Add onions, celery, red pepper, spring onions and
garlic. Cook over a moderate heat for about 3 minutes to
soften the vegetables. Stir in the white pepper, cayenne
pepper and black pepper, dill and parsley.

3. Remove from the heat, add the breadcrumbs and
gradually beat in the egg, adding just enough to hold the
stuffing ingredients together. Season with salt.

4. Stuff the cavity of each trout with an equal amount of the
stuffing and place the trout in a baking dish.

Step 5 Spoon
some of the
stuffing into the
cavity of each fish.

5. Spoon over the remaining butter and bake, uncovered,
in a pre-heated 180°C/350°F/Gas Mark 4 oven for about 25
minutes. Brown under a pre-heated grill before serving, if
desired.

Cook's Notes

Time
Preparation takes about 30
minutes and cooking takes
about 30 minutes.

Variation
Other varieties of fish, such as
sea bass or grey mullet can
also be used.

SERVES 4

PRAWN PROVENÇALE

Deceptively simple, this dish combines all
the ingredients that are easy to find and
that almost everyone enjoys.

60ml/4 tbsps oil
2 large green peppers, seeded and cut into 2.5cm/1
  inch pieces
3 sticks celery, sliced
2 medium onions, diced
2 cloves garlic, crushed
2 400g/14oz cans tomatoes
2 bay leaves
Pinch salt and pepper
Pinch thyme
30g/2 tbsps cornflour mixed with 45ml/3 tbsps dry white
  wine
450g/1lb cooked, peeled prawns

1. Place the oil in a large saucepan and add the
vegetables. Cook for a few minutes over gentle heat and
add the garlic.

2. Add the tomatoes and their juice, breaking up the
tomatoes with a fork or a potato masher. Add the bay
leaves, cayenne pepper or tabasco, seasoning and
thyme, and bring to the boil. Allow to simmer for about 5
minutes, uncovered.

3. Mix a few spoonfuls of the hot tomato liquid with the
cornflour mixture and then return it to the saucepan. Bring
to the boil, stirring constantly until thickened.

4. Simmer over gentle heat for about 15 minutes. Add the
prawns and heat through gently for 5 minutes.

5. Remove the bay leaves before serving, and spoon the
sauce over rice.

Step 1 Cook the vegetables and garlic briefly in hot oil to soften slightly.

Step 3 Mix a few spoonfuls of the hot tomato liquid into the cornflour mixture and then return to the saucepan.

Step 4 Add prawns to the tomato sauce and cook until they curl up and turn pink.

Cook's Notes

Time
Preparation takes about 25
minutes and cooking takes
about 20-30 minutes. Rice will take
about 10-12 minutes to boil.

Cook's Tip
Do not allow prawns or other
shellfish to cook too rapidly or
for too long, as this will toughen them.

Variation
An equal amount of cooked
white fish or even boned and
cooked chicken can be substituted for
the prawns.

SERVES 4

SKATE IN BUTTER SAUCE

This is a lovely tasting fish that
is often neglected. Once you try it,
though, you'll serve it often.

4 wings of skate
1 slice onion
2 parsley stalks
Pinch salt
6 black peppercorns

Beurre Noir

60g/4 tbsps butter
30ml/2 tbsps white wine vinegar
15ml/1 tbsp capers
15ml/1 tbsp chopped parsley (optional)

1. Place the skate in one layer in a large, deep pan. Completely cover with water and add the onion, parsley stalks, salt and peppercorns. Bring gently to the boil with pan uncovered. Allow to simmer 15-20 minutes, or until the skate is done.

2. Lift the fish out onto a serving dish and remove the skin and any large pieces of bone. Take care not to break up the fish.

3. Place the butter in a small pan and cook over high heat until it begins to brown. Add the capers and immediately remove the butter from the heat. Add the vinegar, which will cause the butter to bubble. Add parsley, if using, and pour immediately over the fish to serve.

Step 1 Place the skate in a pan with the poaching liquid and flavouring ingredients.

Step 2 Carefully remove any skin or large bones from the cooked fish, with a small knife.

Step 3 Pour sizzling butter over the fish to serve.

Cook's Notes

Variations
Chopped black olives, shallots or mushrooms may be used instead of or in addition to the capers. Add lemon juice instead of vinegar, if desired.

Cook's Tip
When the skate is done, it will pull away from the bones in long strips.

Time
Preparation takes about 20 minutes, cooking takes 15-20 minutes for the fish and about 5 minutes to brown the butter.

SERVES 4

PIQUANT FRIED FISH

These fish, have a crispy crumb coating
and the fresh tang of lemon juice.

8 sole or plaice fillets
Seasoned flour for dredging
2 eggs, lightly beaten
Dry breadcrumbs
Oil for shallow frying
90g/6 tbsps butter
1 clove garlic, crushed
10ml/2 tsps chopped parsley
30ml/2 tbsps capers
5ml/1 tsp chopped fresh oregano
Juice of 1 lemon
Salt and pepper
Lemon wedges and parsley to garnish

1. Skin the fillets with a sharp filleting knife and remove any small bones.

2. Dredge the fillets lightly with the seasoned flour.

3. Dip the fillets into the beaten eggs to coat, or use a pastry brush to brush the eggs onto the fillets. Dip the egg-coated fillet into the breadcrumbs, pressing the crumbs on firmly.

4. Heat the oil in a large frying pan. Add the fillets and cook slowly on both sides until golden brown. Cook for about 3 minutes on each side, remove and drain on paper towels.

5. Pour the oil out of the frying pan and wipe it clean. Add the butter and the garlic and cook until both turn a light brown. Add the herbs, capers and lemon juice and pour immediately over the fish. Garnish with lemon wedges and sprigs of parsley.

Step 1 Hold each fillet firmly by the tail end and work a sharp filleting knife down the length of the fillet, holding the knife at a slight angle. Keep the blade as close as possible to the fish.

Step 3 Dip or brush the fillets with the beaten egg and press on the breadcrumb coating firmly.

Cook's Notes

Time
Cooking takes about 6 minutes. It may be necessary to cook the fish in several batches, depending upon the size of the frying pan.

Cook's Tip
If necessary, keep the fish fillets warm by placing on a wire cooling rack covered with paper towels and place in a warm oven, leaving the door slightly ajar. Sprinkling the fish fillets lightly with salt as they drain on paper towels helps remove some of the oil.

Variations
Other whitefish fillets may be prepared in the same way. Choose fillets that are of even size so that they cook in the same length of time. Chopped onion may be substituted for the garlic, if desired.

SERVES 4

SWORDFISH WITH GRAPEFRUIT SALAD

Rich and dense in texture, swordfish takes very well to
a tart grapefruit accompaniment.

4-6 ruby or pink grapefruit (depending on size)
1 lime
1 spring onion, finely chopped
30ml/2 tbsps chopped fresh coriander or parsley
15g/1 tbsp sugar
4-8 swordfish steaks (depending on size)
Juice of 1 lime
30ml/2 tbsps oil
Black pepper to taste
Coriander sprigs for garnish

1. Remove the zest from the grapefruit and lime with a zester and set it aside.

2. Remove all the pith from the grapefruit and segment them. Mix the grapefruit and citrus zests with the onion, coriander, sugar and lime juice and set aside.

3. Mix remaining lime juice, oil and pepper together and brush both sides of the fish. Place under a pre-heated grill and cook for about 4 minutes each side depending on distance from the heat source.

4. To serve, place a coriander sprig on each fish steak and serve with the grapefruit.

Step 1 Remove the zest from the grapefruit with a zester.

Step 2 Use a serrated fruit knife to remove all the pith from the grapefruit.

Cook's Notes

Time
Preparation takes about 35 minutes and cooking takes about 4-6 minutes.

Preparation
The amount of sugar needed will vary depending on the sweetness of the grapefruit.

Cook's Tip
For extra flavour, the swordfish steaks may be marinated in a lime juice and oil mixture for up to 1 hour.

SERVES 4

PAN FRIED TROUT

Trout is so delicious that simple preparation
is all that's necessary. Crisp cornmeal, bacon and
pine nuts complement the fresh flavour.

90-120ml/3-4 fl oz vegetable oil
60g/4 tbsps pine nuts
8 rashers streaky bacon, diced
140g/4 oz yellow cornmeal
Pinch salt and white pepper
4 trout weighing about 225g/8oz each, cleaned
Juice of 1 lime
Fresh sage or coriander

Step 3 Dredge the fish with the cornmeal mixture, shaking off any excess.

1. Heat 90ml/6 tbsps of the oil in a large frying pan. Add the pine nuts and cook over moderate heat, stirring constantly. When a pale golden brown, remove them with a draining spoon to paper towels.

2. Add the diced bacon to the oil and cook until crisp, stirring constantly. Drain with the pine nuts.

3. Mix the cornmeal, salt and pepper, and dredge the fish well, patting on the cornmeal. Shake off any excess.

4. If necessary, add more oil to the pan – it should come about halfway up the sides of the fish. Re-heat over moderately high heat.

5. When hot, add the fish two at a time and fry until golden brown, about 4-5 minutes. Turn over and reduce the heat slightly if necessary and cook a further 4-5 minutes. Drain and repeat with the remaining fish.

6. Drain almost all the oil from the pan and re-heat the bacon and the nuts very briefly. Add the lime juice and cook a few seconds. Spoon the bacon and pine nut mixture over the fish and garnish with coriander or sage.

Step 5 Place the fish two at a time in hot oil and fry until golden brown on one side, then turn.

Step 6 Spoon the bacon, pine nut and lime juice mixture over the fish.

Cook's Notes

Time
Preparation takes about 25 minutes and cooking takes about 15-20 minutes.

Preparation
When coating fish, seafood or chicken for frying, prepare just before ready to cook. If the food stands with its coating for too long before cooking, the coating will become soggy.

Variation
If desired, the trout may be dredged with plain or wholemeal flour instead of the cornmeal.

SERVES 4

SNAPPER WITH FENNEL AND ORANGE SALAD

This makes a lovely summer meal. Substitute another
kind of fish if you can't get snapper.

Oil
4 even-sized red snapper, cleaned, heads and tails on
2 heads fennel
2 oranges
Juice of 1 lemon
45ml/3 tbsps light salad oil
Pinch sugar, salt and black pepper

Step 1 Make three cuts in the side of each fish for even cooking.

1. Brush both sides of the fish with oil and cut three slits in the sides of each. Sprinkle with a little of the lemon juice, reserving the rest.

2. Slice the fennel in half and remove the cores. Slice thinly. Also slice the green tops and chop the feathery herb to use in the dressing.

3. Peel the oranges, removing all the white pith.

4. Cut the oranges into segments. Peel and segment over

a bowl to catch the juice.

5. Add lemon juice to any orange juice collected in the bowl. Add the oil, salt, pepper and a pinch of sugar, if necessary. Mix well and add the fennel, green herb tops and orange segments, stirring carefully. Grill the fish 3-5 minutes per side, depending on thickness. Serve the fish with the heads and tails on, accompanied by the salad.

Step 2 Slice the fennel in half and remove the cores.

Step 4 Peel and segment the oranges over a bowl to catch the juice.

Cook's Notes

Time
Preparation takes about 30 minutes and cooking takes about 6-10 minutes.

Variation
Substitute red mullet or any of the exotic fish from the Seychelles. Whole trout can also be used.

Cook's Tip
When grilling whole fish, making several cuts on the side of each fish will help to cook it quickly and evenly throughout.

SERVES 4-6

FISHERMAN'S STEW

This quick, economical and satisfying
fish dish will please any fish lover
for lunch or a light supper.

90ml/6 tbsps olive oil
2 large onions, sliced
1 red pepper, seeded and sliced
120g/4oz mushrooms, sliced
450g/1lb canned tomatoes
Pinch salt and pepper
Pinch dried thyme
430ml/¾ pint water
900g/2lb white fish fillets, skinned
140ml/¼ pint white wine
30ml/2 tbsps chopped parsley

1. Heat the oil in a large saucepan and add the onions. Cook until beginning to look transluscent. Add the pepper and cook until the vegetables are softened.

2. Add the mushrooms and the tomatoes and bring the mixture to the boil.

3. Add thyme, salt, pepper and water and simmer for about 30 minutes.

4. Add the fish and wine and cook until the fish flakes easily, about 15 minutes. Stir in parsley.

5. To serve, place a piece of toasted French bread in the bottom of the soup bowl and spoon over the fish stew.

Use a sharp knife to cut the onion into thin cross-ways slices.

Step 1 Cook the onions in the oil along with the peppers until soft.

Cook's Notes

Time
Preparation takes about 20 minutes and cooking takes about 45 minutes.

Variation
Shellfish may be added with the fish, if desired. Substitute green peppers for red peppers.

Serving Ideas
The stew may also be served over rice. Accompany with a green salad.

SERVES 4

SWORDFISH FLORENTINE

Swordfish has an almost "meaty" texture.
Here it has a distinctly Mediterranean flavour.

4 swordfish steaks about 180-225g/6-8oz each in weight
Salt, pepper and lemon juice
Olive oil
900g/2lbs fresh spinach, stems removed and leaves well
washed

Garlic Mayonnaise

2 egg yolks
1-2 cloves garlic
Salt, pepper and dry mustard
Pinch cayenne pepper
280ml/½ pint olive oil
Lemon juice or white wine vinegar

1. Sprinkle fish with pepper, lemon juice and olive oil. Place under a pre-heated grill and cook for about 3-4 minutes per side. Fish may also be cooked on an outdoor barbeque grill.

2. Meanwhile, use a sharp knife to shred the spinach finely. Place in a large saucepan and add a pinch of salt. Cover and cook over moderate heat with only the water that clings to the leaves after washing. Cook about 2 minutes, or until leaves are just slightly wilted. Set aside.

3. Place egg yolks in a food processor, blender or cup of a hand blender. Add the garlic, crushed, if using a hand blender. Process several times to mix eggs and purée garlic. Add salt, pepper, mustard and cayenne pepper. With the machine running, pour oil through the funnel in a thin, steady stream. Follow manufacturer's directions if using a hand blender.

4. When the sauce becomes very thick, add some lemon juice or vinegar in small quantities.

5. To serve, place a bed of spinach on a plate and top with the swordfish. Spoon some of the garlic mayonnaise on top of the fish and serve the rest separately.

Step 3 Pour the oil for the sauce onto the egg yolks in a thin, steady stream.

Cook's Notes

Time
Preparation takes about 25 minutes and cooking takes about 6-8 minutes.

Variation
Fresh tuna or halibut may be used in place of the swordfish. Even cod goes well with the sauce and spinach.

Preparation
The garlic mayonnaise may be prepared in advance and will keep for 5-7 days in the refrigerator. It is also delicious served with poached shellfish, chicken or vegetables. If too thick, thin the sauce with hot water.

SERVES 4

WHOLE BAKED STUFFED FISH

A whole fish, perfectly cooked, never fails to impress. With a delicious stuffing,
it is certainly grand enough for an important dinner party.

2kg/4¼lb whole fish, gutted and boned (use salmon,
salmon trout or sea bass)

Stuffing

225g/8oz savoury biscuit crumbs
60g/4 tbsps butter, melted
Pinch salt and pepper
10ml/2 tsps lemon juice
1.25ml/¼ tsp each dried thyme, sage and marjoram
1 shallot, finely chopped
120g/4oz button mushrooms, chopped

Step 3 Spoon the stuffing into the cavity of the fish.

Step 2 Place the prepared fish on lightly-greased foil, shiny side up.

Step 4 Pat the fish to distribute the stuffing evenly.

1. Have the fishmonger gut and bone the fish, leaving on the head and tail. Rinse the fish inside and pat dry.

2. Place the fish on lightly oiled foil. Combine all the stuffing ingredients.

3. Open the cavity of the fish and spoon in the stuffing.

4. Close the fish and pat out gently so that the stuffing is evenly distributed. Close the foil loosely around the fish and place it directly on the oven shelf or in a large roasting pan. Cook at 200°C/400°F/Gas Mark 6 for about 40 minutes. Unwrap the fish and slide it onto a serving plate. Peel off the top layer of skin if desired and garnish with lemon slices.

Cook's Notes

Time
Preparation takes about 25 minutes and cooking takes about 40 minutes.

Preparation
If asked, the fishmonger will gut and bone the fish for you. Fish may also be stuffed with the bone in, but this makes it more difficult to serve.

Variation
Add chopped celery or red or green pepper to the stuffing, if desired.

SERVES 4

GRILLED TROUT WITH PEPPER RELISH

Fresh trout, perfectly grilled, and spicy sweet pepper relish
make an unusual, innovative and very special dish.

1 lime
30g/2 tbsps butter, melted
4 filleted trout, unskinned (double fillets preferred)
120g/8 tbsps prepared hot pepper relish
Lime wedges or coriander leaves to garnish

Step 3 Place fillets on a grill and baste with the butter and lime juice mixture.

1. Remove the rind of the lime with a citrus zester and set it aside.

2. Squeeze the juice and mix with the butter.

3. Place the fish fillets on a grill rack and baste with the butter and lime juice mixture. Place under a pre-heated grill for about 4-5 minutes, depending on the thickness of the fillets. Baste frequently.

4. Pour over any remaining butter and lime juice and sprinkle the fish with the lime zest.

5. Gently re-heat the relish and spoon 30ml/2 tbsps down the centre of each of the double fillets. Garnish with lime or coriander.

Step 4 Sprinkle the fish with the lime zest.

Step 5 Spoon the pepper relish down the centre of the double fillets.

Cook's Notes

Time
Preparation takes about 20 minutes if using pre-prepared pepper relish.

Watchpoint
When re-heating the pepper relish, watch it closely as it has a high quantity of sugar and can burn easily.

4

MEAT DISHES

pages 106-157

SERVES 6

BARBECUED PORK LOIN

This versatile sauce keeps well
in the refrigerator and can brighten
up chicken or plain chops, too.

2kg/4½lbs pork loin
280ml/½ pint tomato ketchup
10ml/2 tsps mustard powder
60ml/4 tbsps Worcester sauce
30ml/2 tbsps vinegar
60ml/4 tbsps brown sugar
Half a small onion, finely chopped
60ml/4 tbsps water
Salt (if necessary)

Step 3 Uncover
the ribs and pour
over the sauce.

Step 1 Cook the
pork in a roasting
pan at a high
temperature for 15
minutes.

Step 4 To serve,
cut the ribs into
individual pieces
between the
bones.

1. Place the pork in a roasting pan and cover with foil. Cook for 15 minutes at 220°C/425°F/Gas Mark 8.

2. Meanwhile, combine all the sauce ingredients in a heavy-based pan and bring to the boil. Reduce heat and simmer for about 15 minutes.

3. Reduce the oven temperature to 180°C/350°F/Gas

Mark 4 and uncover the ribs. Pour over the sauce and bake a further hour, basting frequently.

4. Remove the ribs from the roasting pan and reserve the sauce. Place the ribs on a cutting board and slice into individual rib pieces, between the bones.

5. Skim any fat from the surface of the sauce and serve the sauce separately.

Cook's Notes

Time
Preparation takes about 30 minutes and cooking takes about 1 hour 15 minutes.

Serving Ideas
Serve with crusty bread and a salad.

SERVES 6-8

CHILLI BEEF STEW

Beef, red onions, red peppers, paprika,
tomatoes and red beans all go
into this zesty stew.

900g/2lbs beef chuck, cut into 2.5cm/1 inch pieces
Oil
1 large red onion, coarsely chopped
2 cloves garlic, crushed
2 red peppers, seeded and cut into 2.5cm/1 inch pieces
1-2 red chillies, seeded and finely chopped
45ml/3 tbsps mild chilli powder
15ml/1 tbsp cumin
15ml/1 tbsp paprika
700ml/1½ pints beer, water or stock
225g/8oz canned tomatoes, puréed
30ml/2 tbsps tomato purée
225g/8oz canned red kidney beans, drained
Pinch salt
6 ripe tomatoes, peeled, seeded and diced

1. Pour about 60ml/4 tbsps oil into a large saucepan or flameproof casserole. When hot, brown the meat in small batches over moderately high heat for about 5 minutes per batch.

2. Set aside the meat on a plate or in the lid of the casserole. Lower the heat and cook the onion, garlic, red peppers and chillies for about 5 minutes. Add the chilli powder, cumin and paprika and cook for 1 minute further. Pour on the liquid and add the canned tomatoes, tomato purée and the meat.

3. Cook slowly for about 1½-2 hours. Add the beans about 45 minutes before the end of cooking time.

4. When the meat is completely tender, add salt to taste and serve garnished with the diced tomatoes.

Step 2 Cook the onions, garlic, red peppers and chillies slowly until slightly softened.

Step 2 If using beer, add it very slowly as it will tend to foam up in the heat of the pan.

Cook's Notes

 Time
Preparation takes about 25 minutes and cooking takes about 1½-2 hours.

 Freezing
The chilli may be frozen for up to 3 months in a tightly covered freezer container. Allow the chilli to cool completely before sealing and freezing. Defrost in the refrigerator and bring slowly to the boil before serving.

 Variation
The chilli may be made with pork shoulder, with a mixture of beef and pork or minced beef or pork.

SERVES 4

TOMATO BEEF STIR-FRY

East meets West in a dish that is
lightning-fast to cook and tastes
like a "barbeque" sauced stir fry.

450g/1lb sirloin or rump steak
2 cloves garlic, crushed
90ml/6 tbsps wine vinegar
90ml/6 tbsps oil
Pinch sugar, salt and pepper
1 bay leaf
15ml/1 tbsp ground cumin
1 small red pepper, seeded and sliced
1 small green pepper, seeded and sliced
60g/2oz baby sweetcorn
4 spring onions, shredded
Oil for frying

Tomato Sauce

8 fresh ripe tomatoes, peeled, seeded and chopped
60ml/4 tbsps oil
1 medium onion, finely chopped
1-2 green chillies, finely chopped
1-2 cloves garlic, crushed
6 sprigs fresh coriander
45ml/3 tbsps tomato purée

Step 1 Slice the meat thinly across the grain.

1. Slice the meat thinly across the grain. Combine in a plastic bag with the next 6 ingredients. Tie the bag and toss the ingredients inside to coat. Place in a bowl and leave about 4 hours.

2. Heat the oil for the sauce and cook the onion, chillies and garlic to soften but not brown. Add remaining sauce ingredients and cook about 15 minutes over gentle heat. Purée in a food processor until smooth.

3. Heat a frying pan and add the meat in three batches, discarding the marinade. Cook to brown and set aside. Add about 30ml/2 tbsps of oil and cook the peppers about 2 minutes. Add the corn and onions and return the meat to the pan. Cook a further 1 minute and add the sauce. Cook to heat through and serve immediately.

Step 3 Cook the meat quickly over high heat to brown.

Step 3 Add the remaining ingredients and enough sauce to coat all ingredients thoroughly.

Cook's Notes

Time
Preparation takes about 25 minutes, with 4 hours for marinating the meat. The sauce takes about 15 minutes to cook and the remaining ingredients need about 6-7 minutes.

Preparation
The sauce may be prepared ahead of time and kept in the refrigerator for several days. It may also be frozen. Defrost the sauce at room temperature and then boil rapidly to reduce it again slightly.

SERVES 4 or 8

GAMMON STEAKS WITH RAISIN SAUCE

The tart and sweet flavour of this sauce is the
perfect choice to complement gammon.

8 slices smoked or green gammon, cut about 5mm/
   ¼ inch thick
Milk
Oil or margarine for frying
Sauce
25g/1½ tbsps cornflour
280ml/½ pint apple cider
2.5ml/½ tsp ginger or allspice
10ml/2 tsps lemon juice
60g/2oz raisins
Pinch salt

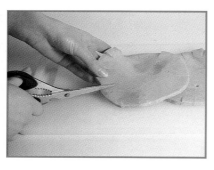

Step 2 Before frying the ham, snip the edges at intervals of 1.25cm/½ inch with kitchen scissors. This will prevent the ham slices from curling.

1. Soak the ham slices in enough milk to barely cover for at least 30 minutes. Rinse and pat dry. Trim off the rind and discard it.

2. Heat a small amount of oil or margarine in a large frying pan and brown the ham slices about 2 minutes per side over medium-high heat.

3. Mix the cornflour with about 90ml/6 tbsps of the apple cider and deglaze the frying pan with the remaining cider. Stir in the ginger or allspice and the lemon juice.

4. Stirring constantly, pour in the cornflour mixture and bring the liquid to the boil. Cook and stir constantly until thickened. Add the raisins and cook a further 5 minutes. Add salt to taste. Reheat the ham quickly, if necessary, and pour over the sauce to serve.

Step 3 Pour the apple cider into the hot pan and scrape to remove any browned meat juices.

Step 4 When the raisins are added to the sauce, cook a further five minutes, or until the raisins are plumped and softened.

Cook's Notes

Time
Preparation takes about 20 minutes with at least 30 minutes soaking in milk for the ham. Cooking takes about 2 minutes per side for the ham and about 10 minutes for the sauce.

Variations
If desired, cooked ham slices or steaks may be used in place of the smoked or green gammon. In this case, omit the soaking procedure and simply fry to brown lightly about 1-2 minutes per side. The apple cider you use may be dry or sweet. If using dry cider, a pinch of sugar will add to the flavour.

Cook's Tip
Soaking smoked or green gammon in milk will help to remove the saltiness, giving it an improved, milder flavour.

SERVES 2

CHOPS IN A PARCEL

Use this quick and easy recipe to
make a whole meal in one convenient
parcel anytime.

2 lamb steaks or 4 rib chops
Oil
1 large potato, scrubbed
4 baby carrots, scraped
1 medium onion, peeled and sliced
1 medium green pepper, seeded and sliced
15ml/1 tbsp chopped fresh dill
Salt and pepper

Step 1 Quickly seal and brown the lamb chops in a small amount of oil over high heat.

1. Heat a frying pan and add a small amount of oil. Quickly fry the lamb on both sides to sear and brown.

2. Cut 2 pieces of foil about 30 x 45cm/12 x 18". Lightly oil the foil.

3. Cut the potatoes in half and place half on each piece of foil, cut side up.

4. Top with the lamb and place the carrots on either side.

5. Place the onion slices on the lamb and the pepper slices on top of the onions.

6. Sprinkle with dill, salt and pepper, and seal into parcels.

7. Bake at 200°C/400°F for about 45 minutes-1 hour, or until the potatoes are tender and the meat is cooked. Open the parcels at the table.

Step 3 Place half a potato on each piece of lightly-oiled foil, cut side up, and place on remaining ingredients.

Step 6 Sprinkle with salt, pepper and dill and seal into parcels.

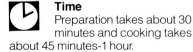
Cook's Notes

 **Time**
Preparation takes about 30 minutes and cooking takes about 45 minutes-1 hour.

 Variation
Other vegetables may be added or substituted. Use sliced parsnips in place of or in addition to the carrots. Substitute a red pepper for the green pepper. Pork chops may also be used, and the cooking time increased by about 15 minutes.

Serving Ideas
This dish is really a complete meal in itself, but add a tomato or green salad for an accompaniment, if desired.

SERVES 8-10

COLA GLAZED HAM

Don't be afraid to try this somewhat
unusual approach to roast ham. Cola
gives it a marvelous taste and colour.

4.5kg/10lb joint smoked gammon
1150ml/2 pints cola soft drink
Whole cloves
225g/8oz dark brown sugar

Step 2 Place the ham rind side down in a roasting pan, pour over the cola and bake.

1. Soak the ham overnight.

2. Preheat oven to 180°C/350°F/Gas Mark 4. Place the ham rind side down in a roasting pan. Pour over all but 90ml/6 tbsps of the cola and bake, uncovered, 1½ hours or until the internal temperature registers 70°C/140°F.

3. Baste the ham every 20 minutes with pan juices using a large spoon or a bulb baster.

4. Remove the ham from the oven and allow it to cool for 10-15 minutes. Remove the rind from the ham with a small, sharp knife and score the fat to a depth of 5mm/¼ inch. Stick 1 clove in the centre of every other diamond.

5. Mix sugar and the remaining cola together and pour or spread over the ham. Raise the oven temperature to 190°C/375°F/Gas Mark 5.

6. Return the ham to the oven and bake for 45 minutes, basting every 15 minutes. Cover loosely with foil if the ham begins to brown too much.

7. Allow to stand 15 minutes before slicing.

Step 4 Remove the rind from the ham with a small sharp knife. Stick one clove in the centre of every other diamond after scoring the fat.

Step 5 Pour or spread the glaze over the ham before continuing to bake.

Cook's Notes

Time
Preparation takes about 30 minutes, with overnight soaking for the ham. Cooking takes about 2 hours 15 minutes.

Serving Ideas
Glazed ham is especially nice served with the Sweet Potato Pudding or Okra Fritters.

Preparation
Many gammon hams require overnight soaking to remove saltiness.

SERVES 4

LAMB STEAKS MEDITERRANEAN STYLE

Aubergine is a very popular vegetable in
Mediterranean cooking. Its taste is perfect with
lamb marinated with garlic and rosemary.

4 large or 8 small round bone lamb steaks
60ml/4 tbsps olive oil
1 clove garlic, crushed
1 sprig fresh rosemary
Black pepper
5ml/1 tbsp red wine vinegar
1 large aubergine
Salt
1 small green pepper, seeded and cut into 2.5cm/1"
   pieces
1 small red pepper, seeded and cut into 2.5cm/1" pieces
2 shallots, chopped
60ml/4 tbsps olive oil
10ml/2 tsps chopped parsley
10ml/2 tsps chopped fresh marjoram
90ml/6 tbsps dry white wine
Salt and pepper

1. Place lamb in a shallow dish with the oil, garlic, rosemary, pepper and vinegar and turn frequently to marinate for 1 hour.

2. Cut the aubergine in half and score lightly. Sprinkle with salt and leave to stand on paper towels for about 30 minutes. Rinse well and pat dry.

3. Cut aubergine in 2.5cm/1" pieces. Heat more oil in a frying pan and add the aubergine. Cook, stirring frequently, over moderate heat until lightly browned. Add peppers, shallots and herbs, and cook a further 5 minutes. Set the mixture aside.

4. Meanwhile, place the lamb on a grill pan, reserving the marinade. Cook under a pre-heated grill for 10 minutes per side. Baste frequently with the marinade. Lamb may be served pink inside.

5. Serve the lamb with the aubergine accompaniment.

Step 2 Cut aubergines in half, score lightly and sprinkle with salt.

Step 4 Boil the wine and vegetables rapidly to reduce the liquid and concentrate flavours.

Cook's Notes

Time
Preparation takes about 1 hour and cooking takes about 20 minutes.

Preparation
Lamb may be marinated overnight.

Cook's Tip
Sprinkling an aubergine with salt will draw out bitter juices and so give the dish better flavour.

SERVES 4

CORNED BEEF HASH

The addition of cooked beetroot
gives this dish a dash of colour.

450g/1lb canned corned beef
3-4 cold boiled potatoes, roughly chopped
1 medium onion, finely chopped
Salt, pepper and nutmeg
1-2 cooked beetroot, peeled and diced
30g/2 tbsps butter or bacon fat

Step 2 Spread out the mixture in the hot fat in a frying pan.

Step 1 Best results are obtained by chopping the meat into small dice by hand.

Step 4 When a crust forms on the bottom, turn the mixture over to brown the other side.

1. Cut the corned beef into small pieces. Combine all the remaining ingredients except the butter or bacon fat.

2. Melt the butter or fat in a frying pan and, when foaming, place in the mixture. Spread it out evenly in the pan.

3. Cook over low heat, pressing the mixture down continuously with a wooden spoon or fish slice. Cook about 15-20 minutes.

4. When a crust forms on the bottom, turn over and brown the other side. Cut into wedges and remove from the pan to serve.

Cook's Notes

Time
Preparation takes about 20 minutes if using leftover corned beef and potatoes from the New England Boiled Dinner recipe. Cooking takes about 25-30 minutes.

Serving Ideas
A freshly-poached egg may be placed on top of each serving of Corned Beef Hash. Serve with a mixture of mustard and horseradish, or horseradish and sour cream.

SERVES 6-8

LAMB STEW

A recipe very similar to the country stews
of France, this one makes use of the often
neglected cut of lamb neck fillet.

1.5kg/3lbs lamb neck fillet, cut into 7.5cm/3 inch pieces
280ml/½ pint dry red wine
280ml/½ pint stock
60ml/4 tbsps red wine vinegar
1 bay leaf
5ml/1 tsp dried thyme
6 black peppercorns
1 clove garlic, crushed
60ml/4 tbsps oil
2 carrots, cut into strips
1 onion, thinly sliced
2 sticks celery, cut into strips
225g/8oz mushrooms, sliced
Chopped parsley to garnish

1. Combine the wine, stock, vinegar, bay leaf, thyme, peppercorns and garlic with the lamb, and marinate about 4 hours.

2. Remove the meat from the marinade and pat dry on paper towels. Reserve the marinade for later use.

3. Heat the oil in a heavy frying pan or casserole and brown the lamb on all sides over high heat. Brown in several small batches if necessary. Remove the lamb and lower the heat. If using a frying pan, transfer the lamb to an ovenproof casserole.

4. Lower the heat and brown the vegetables in the oil until golden. Sprinkle over the flour and cook until the flour browns lightly. Combine the vegetables with the lamb and add the reserved marinade.

5. Cover and cook the stew in a pre-heated 160°C/300°F/Gas Mark 2 oven for about 2 hours.

6. Fifteen minutes before the end of cooking time, add the mushrooms and continue cooking until the meat is tender. Garnish with parsley before serving.

Step 1 Combine the lamb, wine, vinegar, herbs and spices in a polythene bag and tie securely. Place in a bowl to catch any drips and turn the bag often to marinate evenly.

Step 4 When the vegetables and flour have browned, combine them with the browned meat. Gradually pour marinade over the ingredients, stirring well.

Cook's Notes

 Time
Preparation takes about 30 minutes, plus marinating. Cooking takes about 10 minutes for the meat to brown and about 2 hours for the stew to cook.

Preparation
The stew may be prepared in advance and refrigerated, which will intensify the flavour. Reheat slowly, but bring briefly to the boil before serving.

 Serving Ideas
Serve with mashed or boiled potatoes. Add a green vegetable or salad if desired.

SERVES 6-8

POT ROASTED BEEF

An excellent way to cook flavour and
tenderness into economical cuts of beef.

1.5kg/3lb beef roast (rump, chuck, round or top end)
Flour seasoned with salt and pepper
30ml/2 tbsps butter or margarine
1 onion stuck with 2 cloves
1 bay leaf
10ml/2 tsps fresh thyme or 5ml/1 tsp dried thyme
280ml/½ pint beef stock
4 carrots
12 small onions, peeled
4 small turnips, peeled and left whole
2 potatoes, cut into even-sized pieces
30g/2 tbsps butter or margarine mixed with 30g/2 tbsps
    flour

1. Dredge the beef with the seasoned flour, patting off the excess.

2. Melt the butter in a large, heavy-based casserole or saucepan and, when foaming, brown the meat on all sides, turning it with wooden spoons or a fish slice.

3. When well browned, add the onion stock with the cloves, bay leaf and thyme and pour on the stock. Cover the pan, reduce the heat and cook on top of the stove or in a pre-heated 160°C/300°F/Gas Mark 2 oven. Cook slowly for about 2 hours, adding more liquid, either stock or water, as necessary.

4. Test the meat and, if beginning to feel tender, add the vegetables. Cover and continue to cook until the meat is completely tender and the vegetables are cooked through.

5. Remove the meat and vegetables from the casserole or pan and place them on a warm serving platter. Skim the excess fat from the top of the sauce and bring it back to the boil.

6. Mix the butter and flour (beurre manie) to a smooth paste. Add about 5ml/1 tsp of the mixture to the boiling sauce and whisk thoroughly. Continue adding the mixture until the sauce is of the desired thickness. Carve the meat and spoon over some of the sauce. Serve the rest of the sauce separately.

Step 2 Place the meat in the hot fat to brown slowly and evenly. Use wooden spoons or a fish slice to turn.

Step 6 If the sauce needs thickening at the end, add a small spoonful of flour and butter paste and whisk well.

Cook's Notes

Time
Preparation takes about 30 minutes and cooking takes about 2-2½ hours.

Cook's Tip
The flour and butter paste or beurre manie may be prepared in large quantities and kept in the refrigerator or freezer to use any time thickening is necessary for a sauce.

Serving Ideas
This dish can be a meal in itself. If an accompaniment is desired, serve a green vegetable or a salad.

SERVES 4
CURRIED PORK STEW

This savoury stew requires long,
slow cooking to bring out its flavour.

900g/2lb pork shoulder, cut in 5cm/2 inch cubes
Oil
2 medium onions, cut in 5cm/2 inch pieces
1 large green pepper, seeded and cut in 5cm/2 inch
　　pieces
15ml/1 tbsp curry powder
2 cloves garlic, crushed
450g/1lb canned tomatoes
45ml/3 tbsps tomato purée
140ml/¼ pint water or beef stock
30ml/2 tbsps cider vinegar
1 bay leaf
2.5ml/½ tsp dried mint
Salt and a few drops tabasco sauce

Step 1 Brown the pork cubes in oil over high heat in a large frying pan.

Step 2 Combine the ingredients and stir well to break up the tomatoes slightly.

1. Heat about 30ml/2 tbsps oil in a large sauté or frying pan. When hot, add the pork cubes in two batches. Brown over high heat for about 5 minutes per batch. Remove to a plate. Add more oil if necessary and cook the onions and peppers to soften slightly. Add the curry powder and garlic and cook 1 minute more.

2. Add the tomatoes, their juice and the tomato purée. Stir in the water or stock and vinegar breaking up the tomatoes slightly. Add bay leaf, mint and salt.

3. Transfer to a flameproof casserole dish. Bring the mixture to the boil and then cook slowly for about 1½ hours, covered.

4. When the meat is completely tender, skim any fat from the surface of the sauce, remove the bay leaf and add a few drops of tabasco sauce to taste.

Step 4 When the meat is tender, skim excess fat from the surface of the sauce with a spoon, or blot up with strips of paper towel.

Cook's Notes

Time
Preparation takes about 25 minutes and cooking takes about 1½ hours.

Freezing
Allow the stew to cool completely. Spoon into freezer containers, cover tightly and freeze for up to 3 months. Defrost in the refrigerator and then slowly bring to the boil to re-heat before serving.

Serving Ideas
Serve with a spicy pilaff and Nan bread which is available from Indian grocers.

SERVES 4

BOILED SILVERSIDE

The "corning process" for preserving beef was a useful one in the days before refrigerators were commonplace. The process took a long time, but fortunately we can now buy our beef already "corned"!

1.5 kg/3lb corned silverside of beef
1 bay leaf
5ml/1 tsp mustard seed
3 allspice berries
3 cloves
5ml/1 tsp dill seed
6 black peppercorns
2 potatoes, cut into even-sized pieces
4 small onions, peeled
4 large carrots, scraped
4 small or 2 large parsnips, peeled and cut into even-sized pieces
1 large or 2 small swedes
1 medium-size green cabbage, cored and quartered
Salt

1. Place the beef in a large saucepan with enough water to cover and add the bay leaf and spices. Cook for about 2 hours, skimming any foam from the surface as the meat cooks.

2. Add the potatoes and onions and cook for about 15 minutes. Taste and add salt if necessary.

3. Add the carrots, parsnips and swede and cook for a further 15 minutes. Add the cabbage and cook a further 15 minutes.

4. Remove the meat from the casserole and slice it thinly. Arrange on a warm serving platter and remove the vegetables from the broth with a draining spoon, placing them around the meat. Serve immediately with horseradish or mustard.

Step 1 Combine the beef, salted water and spices in the pan. Bring to the boil, skimming the foam that rises to the surface.

Step 3 When the beef and root vegetables have cooked for 15 minutes, add the cabbage, pushing it under the liquid.

Step 4 Remove the meat from the pan and slice thinly across the grain.

Cook's Notes

Preparation
The meat may be cooked for its first 2 hours in advance and refrigerated overnight if desired. Reheat and then add the vegetables according to the recipe.

Time
Preparation takes about 30 minutes and cooking takes about 3 hours.

Variation
Freshly-cooked beetroot may be added to the vegetable selection. Cook the beetroot separately or it will colour all the vegetables and the meat. Substitute turnips for the swede if desired.

SERVES 4

GINGERSNAP PORK CHOPS

Ginger-flavoured biscuits give a spicy lift to pork
chop gravy, thickening it at the same time.

4 even-sized pork chops, loin or shoulder
5ml/1 tsp ground black pepper
Pinch salt
5ml/1 tsp ground ginger
1.25ml/¼ tsp each rubbed sage, ground
   coriander and paprika
Pinch dried thyme
30ml/2 tbsps oil
30g/2 tbsps butter
1 small onion, finely chopped
1 stick celery, finely chopped
½ clove garlic, crushed
430ml/¾ pint chicken stock
12-14 gingersnap biscuits

Step 2 Brown the chops on both sides in the hot oil until golden.

1. Trim the chops if they have excess fat. Mix together the herbs and spices and press the mixture onto the chops firmly on both sides.

2. Heat the oil in a large frying pan and, when hot, add the chops. Brown on both sides and remove to a plate.

3. Add the butter to the frying pan and, when foaming, add the onions, celery and garlic. Cook to soften and pour on the stock.

4. Return the chops to the pan, cover and cook for about 30-40 minutes, or until tender.

5. When the chops are cooked, remove them to a serving dish and keep them warm. Crush the gingersnaps in a food processor. Alternatively, place the gingersnaps in a plastic bag and use a rolling pin to crush them. Stir the crushed gingersnaps into the pan liquid and bring to the boil.

6. Stir constantly to allow the gingersnaps to soften and thicken the liquid. Boil rapidly for about 3 minutes to reduce, and pour over the chops to serve.

Step 5 Use the crushed gingersnaps to thicken the pan liquid. Cook slowly until dissolved.

Cook's Notes

Time
Preparation takes about 20 minutes and cooking takes about 50 minutes.

Variation
Chicken or rabbit may be used in place of the pork.

Cook's Tip
The gingersnaps should thicken the cooking liquid sufficiently. If not, combine 10ml/2 tsps cornflour with 15ml/1 tbsp water and some of the hot cooking liquid. Return to the pan and bring to the boil, stirring constantly until thickened and cleared.

SERVES 8

LAMB AND PEPPER BRAISE

This dish is an ideal way to
use an inexpensive cut of lamb
to its best advantage.

1.5kg/3lb middle neck or other neck cut of lamb
Pinch salt and black pepper
90ml/6 tbsps oil
2 onions, sliced
1 large red pepper, seeded and sliced
2 sticks celery, sliced
90g/6 tbsps flour
2 cloves garlic, crushed
1.5 litres/2½ pints stock or water
30ml/2 tbsps chopped parsley

Step 1 Cut in between the bones to divide the meat into even-size pieces.

1. Cut the lamb between the bones into individual pieces. Sprinkle a mixture of black pepper and salt over the surface of the chops, patting it in well.

2. Heat the oil in a large stock pot or casserole and when hot add the meat, a few pieces at a time, and brown on both sides.

3. When all the meat is brown, remove to a plate and add the onions, pepper and celery to the oil. Lower the heat and cook to soften. Remove and set aside with the meat.

4. Add the flour to the remaining oil in the pan and stir well. Cook slowly until a dark golden brown. Add the garlic and stir in the stock or water. Return the meat and vegetables to the pan or casserole and bring to the boil. Cover and cook slowly for 1½-2 hours, or until the lamb is very tender. Sprinkle with parsley and serve immediately.

Step 1 Mix the salt and pepper together and sprinkle over the surface of the meat, patting in well.

Step 2 Brown the meat, a few pieces at a time, over very high heat.

Cook's Notes

Time
Preparation takes about 25 minutes and cooking takes about 2 hours.

Variation
The braise may be prepared with pork chops, sliced pork loin or with an inexpensive cut of beef.

Preparation
The braise may be prepared in advance and kept in the refrigerator for up to 2 or 3 days. Reheat slowly. Flavours will intensify.

MAKES 8

SPICY MEAT PIES

These meat pies are fried rather
than baked. Add cayenne gradually
to taste.

Pastry

45ml/3 tbsps butter or margarine
2 eggs
60-90ml/4-6 tbsps milk or water
300-400g/10-14oz plain flour
Pinch sugar and salt

Filling

30g/2 tbsps butter or margarine
½ small onion, finely chopped
½ small green pepper, finely chopped
1 stick celery, finely chopped
1 clove garlic, crushed
340g/¾lb minced pork
1 bay leaf, finely crushed
5ml/1 tsp cayenne pepper
Pinch salt
30g/2 tbsps flour
280ml/½ pint beef stock
15ml/1 tbsp tomato purée
5ml/1 tsp dried thyme

Step 7 Spread the filling on half of each pastry circle and brush the edges with water.

Step 8 Fold over and seal the edges together, pressing them firmly. Crimp with a fork.

1. To prepare the pastry, soften the butter or margarine in a food processor or with an electric mixer until creamy. Beat in the eggs one at a time and add the milk or water.

2. Sift in 300g/10oz flour, sugar and salt and mix until blended. If necessary, add the remaining flour gradually until the mixture forms a ball. Wrap well and refrigerate about 30 minutes.

3. Melt the butter or margarine in a large frying pan and cook the onion, pepper, celery, garlic and pork over moderate heat. Break up the meat with a fork as it cooks.

4. Add the bay leaf, cayenne pepper, salt and flour and cook, scraping the bottom of the pan often, until the flour browns.

5. Pour on the stock and stir in the tomato purée and

thyme. Bring to the boil and cook, stirring occasionally, until thickened. Chill thoroughly and remove the bay leaf.

6. Divide the pastry into 8 pieces and roll each out to a circle about 3mm/⅛ inch thick.

7. Spread the chilled filling on half of each circle to within 1.25cm/½ inch of the edge. Brush the edge with water.

8. Fold over and seal the edges together firmly. Crimp the edges with a fork.

9. Heat oil in a deep sauté pan or a deep fat fryer to about 180°C/350°F. Fry 2 or 3 pies at a time for about 2 minutes, holding them under the surface of the oil with a metal spoon to brown evenly. Remove from the oil with a draining spoon and drain on paper towels. Serve immediately.

Cook's Notes

Time
Preparation takes about 30-40 minutes, and cooking takes about 15 minutes for the filling and 2 minutes for each batch of 2 pies.

Cook's Tip
The dough may be prepared in advance and kept in a refrigerator for about 2 days.

Variation
Minced beef may be substituted for the pork. Double the quantity of vegetables for a vegetarian filling.

SERVES 6-8

PORK AND PEPPER STEW

Avocado makes an unusual
but delicious garnish for
this tasty meat stew.

900g/2lbs lean pork, cut into 2.5cm/1inch pieces
Oil
3 green peppers, seeded and cut into 2.5cm/1 inch
 pieces
1-2 green chilli peppers, seeded and finely chopped
1 small bunch spring onions, chopped
2 cloves garlic, crushed
15ml/2 tsps chopped fresh oregano
45ml/3 tbsps chopped fresh coriander
1 bay leaf
700ml/1½ pints chicken stock
225g/8oz canned chickpeas, drained
25g/1½ tbsps cornflour mixed with 45ml/3 tbsps cold
 water (optional)
Salt
1 large ripe avocado, peeled and diced
15ml/1 tbsp lime juice

1. Heat 60ml/4 tbsps of oil and lightly brown the pork
cubes over high heat. Use a large flameproof casserole
and brown the pork in 2 or 3 batches.

2. Lower the heat and cook the peppers to soften slightly.
Add the chillies, onions and garlic and cook for 2 minutes.

3. Add the herbs and liquid and reduce the heat. Simmer,
covered, 1-1½ hours or until the meat is tender. Add the
chickpeas during the last 45 minutes.

4. If necessary, thicken with the cornflour, stirring
constantly after adding until the liquid thickens and clears.

5. Add salt to taste and remove the bay leaf.

6. Toss the avocado in lime juice and sprinkle over the
top of the chilli to serve.

Step 1 The pork
should barely
begin to take on
colour. Do not over
brown.

Step 4 If neces-
sary, add the
cornflour mixture
to thicken, stirring
constantly.

Cook's Notes

Time
Preparation takes about 30-40
minutes and cooking takes
about 1-1½ hours.

Variation
Chicken or lamb make good
alternatives to pork.

Serving Ideas
Delicious with a cucumber
salad.

SERVES 6

SWEET POTATO AND SAUSAGE CASSEROLE

This is a close relative of the soufflé. Although it won't rise as high, it is easier to make!

900g/2lbs sweet potatoes
30ml/2 tbsps oil
225g/8oz sausage meat
1 small onion, finely chopped
2 sticks celery, finely chopped
½ green pepper, finely chopped
Pinch sage and thyme
Pinch salt and pepper
2 eggs, separated

1. Peel the sweet potatoes and cut them into 5cm/2 inch pieces. Place in boiling water to cover and add a pinch of salt. Cook quickly, uncovered, for about 20 minutes or until the sweet potatoes are tender to the point of a knife. Drain them well and leave them to dry.

2. Purée the potatoes using a potato masher.

3. While the potatoes are cooking, heat the oil in a large frying pan and add the sausage meat. Cook briskly, breaking up with a fork until the meat is golden brown. Add the onion, celery and green pepper, and cook for a further 5 minutes. Add the sage, thyme and a pinch of seasoning.

4. Beat the egg yolks into the mashed sweet potatoes and, using an electric mixer or a hand whisk, beat the egg whites until stiff but not dry.

5. Drain any excess fat from the sausage meat and combine it with the sweet potatoes. Fold in the whisked egg whites until thoroughly incorporated. Spoon the mixture into a well-buttered casserole dish or soufflé dish and bake in a preheated 190°C/375°F/Gas Mark 5 oven until well risen and brown on the top, about 25–30 minutes. Serve immediately.

Step 3 Brown the sausage meat in oil, mashing with a fork to break up lumps as the meat cooks.

Step 4 Add the egg yolks to the potato mixture, beating well with a wooden spoon.

Step 4 Whisk the egg whites until stiff but not dry.

Cook's Notes

Time
Preparation takes about 35 minutes and cooking takes a total of 45 minutes.

Serving Ideas
Serve as a side dish with poultry, or on its own as a light main course.

SERVES 4

SPICED LAMB

Tender sautéed lamb is delicious
in a sauce that's fragrant with
herbs and spices.

450g/1lb lamb neck fillet
5ml/1 tsp fresh dill, chopped
5ml/1 tsp rosemary, crushed
5ml/1 tsp thyme, chopped
10ml/2 tsp mustard seeds, crushed slightly
2 bay leaves
5ml/1 tsp coarsely ground black pepper
2.5ml/½ tsp ground allspice
Juice of 2 lemons
280ml/½ pint red wine
30ml/2 tbsps oil
30g/2 tbsps butter or margarine
1 small red pepper, seeded and sliced
90g/3oz button mushrooms, left whole
45g/3 tbsps flour
140ml/¼ pint beef stock
Salt

1. Place the lamb in a shallow dish and sprinkle on the dill, rosemary, thyme and mustard seeds. Add the bay leaves, pepper, allspice, lemon juice and wine, and stir to coat the meat thoroughly with the marinade. Leave for 4 hours in the refrigerator.

2. Heat the oil in a large frying pan and add the red pepper and mushrooms and cook to soften slightly. Remove with a draining spoon.

3. Reheat the oil in the pan and add the lamb fillet, well drained and patted dry. Reserve marinade. Brown meat quickly on all sides to seal. Remove from the pan and set aside with the vegetables.

4. Melt the butter in the pan and when foaming add the flour. Lower the heat and cook the flour slowly until a good, rich brown. Pour in the beef stock and the marinade. Bring to the boil and return the vegetables and lamb to the pan. Cook about 15 minutes, or until the lamb is tender, but still pink inside.

5. Slice the lamb fillet thinly on the diagonal and arrange on plates. Remove the bay leaves from the sauce and spoon over the meat to serve.

Step 1 Place lamb fillet in a shallow dish and mix with the marinating ingredients.

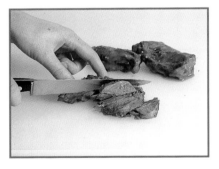

Step 5 To serve, slice lamb fillet on the diagonal with a large, sharp knife or carving knife.

Cook's Notes

Time
Preparation takes about 25 minutes, plus 4 hours marinating time for the meat. Cooking takes about 35 minutes.

Variation
Recipe can be prepared with pork fillet or steak.

Serving Ideas
Serve with rice or Pommes Noisettes (small potato balls browned in butter or sauté potatoes.)

SERVES 4

PORK CHOPS WITH SPRING VEGETABLES

4 pork chops
Oil for frying
15g/1 tbsp butter or margarine
1 carrot, peeled and diced
12 button onions
15g/1 tbsp flour
430ml/¾ pint beef stock
30ml/2 tbsps lemon juice
Salt and pepper
90g/3oz French beans, topped, tailed and sliced
60g/2oz peas

Step 2 Put unpeeled onions into a saucepan of boiling water and bring back to the boil for 1-2 minutes. Transfer to a bowl of cold water.

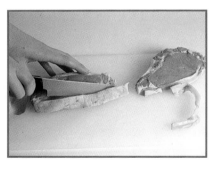

Step 1 Use a small, sharp knife to trim away most of the pork fat.

Step 2 Allow to cool. Peels should come off easily.

1. Heat about 30ml/2 tbsps of the oil in a large frying pan. Trim the chops to remove most of the fat. Fry slowly on both sides in the hot fat until browned, about 15 minutes.

2. Melt the butter or margarine in a medium saucepan. Peel the onions and add to the butter with the carrot. Cook slowly to soften. Sprinkle on the flour and cook to a good golden brown. Add the stock, lemon juice, salt and pepper and bring to the boil. Cook until thick.

3. Pour the fat from the pork and pour in the sauce. Add the beans and peas and cook until the pork is tender, about 35 minutes.

Cook's Notes

Time
Preparation takes about 25 minutes, and cooking takes about 50 minutes.

Variation
Serve the same sauce with beef, chicken or lamb.

Preparation
Brown the flour slowly, stirring constantly for an even colour and to prevent a burned taste.

SERVES 4

BRAISED RABBIT WITH PEPPERS

Rabbit is available fresh from butchers during the season. Otherwise look for it in freezer cabinets in major supermarkets.

1kg/2¼ rabbit joints
1 lemon slice
Flour for dredging
Pinch salt and pepper
5ml/1 tsp dry mustard
5ml/1 tsp paprika
5ml/1 tsp garlic granules
1.25ml/¼ tsp dried dill
Oil for frying
1 onion, thinly sliced
1 small green pepper, seeded and thinly sliced
1 small red pepper, seeded and thinly sliced
1-400g/14oz canned tomatoes
280ml/½ pint chicken stock
60ml/1 tbsps dry white wine or sherry (optional)
1 bay leaf

1. Soak the rabbit overnight with the lemon slice in cold water to cover.

2. Drain the rabbit and pat dry with paper towels.

3. Combine flour, spices, herbs, and seasoning and dredge the rabbit with the mixture.

4. Heat the oil and fry the rabbit on all sides until golden brown. Remove to a plate.

5. Cook the onion and peppers for about 1 minutes. Add the tomatoes, stock and bay leaf and bring to the boil. Return the rabbit to the pan and spoon over the sauce. Partially cover and cook over gentle heat until tender, about 45-50 minutes.

6. Add the wine or sherry during the last 10 minutes of cooking, if using. Remove the bay leaf before serving.

Step 3 Dredge the rabbit in the seasoned flour mixture and shake off the excess.

Step 4 Heat the oil and fry the rabbit on both sides until golden brown.

Step 5 Cook the rabbit in the sauce with the peppers and onions until tender to the point of a knife.

Cook's Notes

Time
Preparation takes about 25 minutes, with overnight soaking for the rabbit. Cooking takes about 50 minutes-1 hour.

Variation
If yellow peppers are available, use the three colours for an attractive dish.

Cook's Tip
Soaking the rabbit with lemon overnight helps to whiten the meat and to remove any strong taste.

SERVES 4

SAUTÉED LEMON PORK

A perfect way to prepare this tender cut of
pork. Butchers will bat out the meat for you.

8 small pork escalopes or steaks, batted out until thin
Flour for dredging
Salt and pepper
30g/2 tbsps butter or margarine
1 green pepper, seeded and thinly sliced
90ml/6 tbsps dry white wine or sherry
15ml/1 tbsp lemon juice
180ml/6 fl oz chicken stock
1 lemon, peeled and thinly sliced

Step 3 Cook the peppers briefly and remove them while still green and slightly crisp.

Step 1 Use a flour dredger to sprinkle flour on the pork. Pat in by hand and then shake the pieces to remove excess flour.

Step 4 Pour the wine or sherry and lemon juice into the hot fat in the pan and scrape to deglaze.

1. Dredge pork with a mixture of flour, salt and pepper. Shake off the excess.

2. Melt the butter or margarine in a large frying pan or sautée pan and brown the pork, a few pieces at a time. Remove the meat and keep it warm.

3. Cook the peppers briefly and set aside with the pork.

4. Pour the wine or sherry and lemon juice into the pan to deglaze. Add the stock and bring to the boil. Boil for 5 minutes to reduce. Add the pork and peppers and cook 15 minutes over gentle heat. Add the lemons and heat through before serving.

Cook's Notes

Time
Preparation takes about 25 minutes and cooking takes about 20-25 minutes.

Variation
Use red pepper instead of green pepper and add chopped spring onions.

SERVES 4

RICH PAN-FRIED STEAKS

Thin steaks are quickly fried and
then cooked in a savoury brown sauce.

4-8 pieces frying steak, depending on size
15ml/1 tbsp oil
15g/1 tbsp butter or margarine
15g/1 tbsp flour
6 spring onions
1 clove garlic, crushed
5ml/1 tsp chopped thyme
10ml/2 tsps chopped parsley
3 tomatoes, peeled, seeded and chopped
280ml/½ pint beef stock
Salt

it finely. Add to the flour and butter, reserving the green tops for later use.

4. Add garlic to the pan and cook the mixture slowly, stirring frequently until it is a dark golden brown. Add the herbs, tomatoes, stock, tabasco and salt to taste and bring to the boil. Cook about 5 minutes to thicken and add the steaks. Cook to heat the meat through.

5. Chop the green tops of the onions and sprinkle over the steaks to garnish.

Step 2 Press the meat against the hot pan to brown it quickly and evenly.

Step 1 Pound the meat with a rolling pin or meat mallet to flatten slightly.

1. Place the meat between 2 sheets of clingfilm or waxed paper and pound with a rolling pin or a meat mallet to flatten slightly.

2. Heat the oil in a large frying pan and brown the meat quickly, a few pieces at a time. Set the meat aside.

3. Melt the butter or margarine in the frying pan and add the flour. Cut the white part off the spring onions and chop

Step 4 Cook the sauce rapidly for about 5 minutes to thicken. Tomatoes will break up slightly.

Cook's Notes

 Time
Preparation takes about 25 minutes and cooking takes about 20 minutes.

 Serving Ideas
Serve with rice or potatoes. Add a green vegetable or salad.

 Variation
Add chopped red or green pepper to the sauce.

SERVES 6-8

BACON AND RED BEAN PILAFF

This is a delicious way to make a small amount of meat go a long way. For convenience, substitute double quantity canned beans.

225g/8oz dried red kidney beans
1 bay leaf
1 sprig thyme
225g/8oz green gammon or bacon
60g/4 tbsps butter or margarine
1 onion, finely chopped
1 green pepper, seeded and cut into small dice
3 sticks celery, finely chopped
2 cloves garlic, crushed
Salt
225g/8oz rice, cooked
4 spring onions, finely chopped

Step 1 Soak the kidney beans in water overnight, until they swell in size.

1. Pick over the beans and place them in a large stockpot or bowl. Cover with water and leave to soak overnight. Drain them and place in a pot of fresh water with the sprig of thyme, bay leaf and a pinch of salt. Add the piece of gammon or bacon and bring to the boil. Partially cover the pan and leave to boil rapidly for 10 minutes. Reduce the heat and then simmer for 2½-3 hours, adding more water if necessary.

2. When the beans have been cooking for about half the required length of time, melt the butter in a small frying pan and cook the onion, pepper, garlic and celery until the onions look translucent. Add this mixture to the beans and continue cooking them.

3. Once the beans are soft, mash some of them against the side of the pot with a large spoon. Alternatively, remove about 180ml/6 fl oz of the mixture and blend to a smooth puree in a food processor or blender. Pour back into the pot to thicken the rest of the beans.

4. Remove the piece of gammon or bacon, trim off excess fat and cut the meat into 1.25cm/½ inch pieces. Return to the beans. Stir well and continue to cook the beans. Remove thyme and bayleaf before serving.

5. To serve, place rice on serving plates and spoon over some of the beans. Sprinkle the top with the chopped spring onion.

Step 3 Once the beans are completely softened, mash some of them against the side of the pot with a large spoon.

Cook's Notes

Time
Preparation takes about 25 minutes, with overnight soaking for the beans. Cooking takes about 2½-3 hours.

Watchpoint
The beans must boil vigorously for the first 10 minutes of cooking time. Make sure that the beans are completely cooked – it can be dangerous to eat dried pulses that are insufficiently cooked.

Variation
Smoked sausage or garlic sausage may be used instead of the gammon or bacon.

SERVES 2-4

SWEET & SOUR PORK

This really needs no introduction because of its
popularity. Now you can make this favourite
Chinese restaurant dish at home.

120g/4oz plain flour
60g/4 tbsps cornflour
7.5ml/1½ tsps baking powder
Pinch salt
15ml/1 tbsp oil
Water
225g/8oz pork fillet, cut into 1.25cm/½ inch cubes

Sweet and Sour Sauce

30g/2 tbsps cornflour
120g/4oz light brown sugar
Pinch salt
120ml/4 fl oz cider vinegar or rice vinegar
1 clove garlic, crushed
5ml/1 tsp fresh ginger, grated
90ml/6 tbsps tomato ketchup
90ml/6 tbsps reserved pineapple juice

1 onion, sliced
1 green pepper, seeded, cored and sliced
1 small can pineapple chunks, juice reserved
Oil for frying

1. To prepare the batter, sift the flour, cornflour, baking
powder and salt into a bowl. Make a well in the centre and
add the oil and enough water to make a thick, smooth
batter. Using a wooden spoon, stir the ingredients in the
well, gradually incorporating flour from the outside, and
beat until smooth.

2. Heat enough oil in a wok to deep-fry the pork. Dip the
pork cubes one at a time into the batter and drop into the hot
oil. Fry 4-5 pieces of pork at a time and remove them with a
draining spoon to paper towels.

3. Pour off most of the oil from the wok and add the sliced
onion, pepper and pineapple. Cook over high heat for 1-2
minutes. Remove and set aside.

4. Mix all the sauce ingredients together and pour into the
wok. Bring slowly to the boil, stirring continuously until
thickened. Allow to simmer for about 1-2 minutes or until
completely clear.

5. Add the vegetables, pineapple and pork cubes to the
sauce and stir to coat completely. Reheat for 1-2 minutes
and serve immediately.

Step 2 Dip the
pork cubes into
the batter and
then drop into the
hot oil. Chopsticks
are ideal to use for
this.

Step 3 Place the
onion half flat on a
chopping board
and use a large,
sharp knife to cut
across to thick or
thin slices as
desired. Separate
these into
individual strips.

Cook's Notes

Time
Preparation takes about 15
minutes, cooking takes about
15 minutes.

Variation
Use beef or chicken instead of
the pork. Uncooked, peeled
prawns may be used as can whitefish,
cut into 2.5cm/1 inch pieces.

Cook's Tip
If pork is prepared ahead of
time, this will have to be refried
before serving to crisp up.

SERVES 8-10

BRAISED OXTAILS

Oxtails are very economical, but rich in flavour. As they cook, they thicken their own sauce, so very little flour is needed.

2kg/4½lbs oxtails
Flour for dredging
Salt and pepper
2 onions, coarsely chopped
1 large green pepper, coarsely chopped
3 sticks celery, coarsely chopped
4 cloves garlic, crushed
900g/2lbs canned tomatoes
570ml/1 pint beef stock
30ml/2 tbsps red wine vinegar
30ml/2 tbsps dark brown sugar
Pinch dried thyme
1 bay leaf
Oil for frying
15ml/1 tbsp Dijon mustard
Chopped parsley

1. Trim excess fat from the oxtails and cut them into 5cm/2 inch pieces.

2. Place a few pieces in a sieve and sprinkle over flour, salt and pepper. Shake the sieve to dredge the pieces of meat lightly in flour and repeat until all pieces are coated.

3. Heat the oil in a large casserole or saucepan and brown the meat in several batches.

4. When all the oxtails are browned, remove them to a plate and add the onion, green pepper, celery and garlic to the pan or casserole. Cook over moderately high heat, stirring until the vegetables have softened but not browned. Return the oxtails to the pan and add the tomatoes, stock, vinegar, brown sugar, thyme, and bay leaf.

5. Bring to the boil and then reduce the heat. Cover and cook gently on top of the stove or in a preheated 180°C/350°F/Gas Mark 4 oven for about 3½ hours, or until the meat is very tender.

6. When the oxtails are cooked, transfer them to a serving dish and remove the bay leaf from the sauce. Skim the fat and purée the vegetables and the sauce in a food processor until smooth. Add the mustard and a pinch of salt, if necessary. Spoon over the oxtails and sprinkle with chopped parsley, if desired.

Step 3 Brown a few pieces of oxtail at a time in hot oil in a casserole or saucepan.

Cook's Notes

Time
Preparation takes about 30 minutes and cooking takes about 3½ hours.

Freezing
The recipe may be prepared in advance and frozen in rigid containers for up to three months. Allow to defrost completely before reheating. Sauce may need whisking to bring it back together once reheated.

Serving Ideas
Serve with freshly boiled rice or with French bread.

SERVES 4

PORK AND PEPPER SAUTÉ

Colourful and slightly spicy
this dish has the taste of
Hungarian goulash.

8 pork escalopes
Seasoned flour
45g/3 tbsps butter or margarine
1 onion
1 red and 1 green pepper, thinly sliced
30g/2 tbsps flour
15ml/1 tbsp paprika
140-280ml/¼-½ pint stock
140ml/¼ pint plain yogurt

Step 3 Slice onion thinly and add to pan. Add the pepper slices and sauté for 3 minutes until soft but not browned.

1. Trim the escalopes to remove any fat. Bat them out if desired. Dredge in the seasoned flour and shake off the excess.

2. Melt the butter or margarine in a large frying pan or sauté pan and, when foaming, place in the escalopes. It may be necessary to cook them in two or four batches. Lower the heat and brown slowly on both sides for about 8 minutes in total. Remove and keep warm.

3. Slice the onion thinly and add to the pan. Add the pepper slices and sauté for about 3 minutes. Remove and set aside with the pork escalopes.

4. Add the flour to the pan and allow it to cook slowly until golden brown. Add the paprika and cook for 1 minute.

5. Whisk in the stock gradually to prevent lumps and bring to the boil. Replace the pork and vegetables, cover and cook for 20–25 minutes, or until the pork is tender.

6. Beat the yogurt until smooth and drizzle over the pork to serve.

Step 6 Beat the yogurt well to remove any lumps and to thin it slightly. If still too thick to run easily from the spoon, add water or milk.

Step 6 Drizzle yogurt onto the pork over the prongs of a fork or over a tea-spoon. If desired, use a knife and swirl the yogurt partially into the sauce.

Cook's Notes

Time
Preparation takes about 30 minutes, cooking takes about 35-40 minutes. Tender cuts of pork dry out very quickly, so brown slowly to avoid toughening.

Preparation
Always remove the white pith from inside the peppers as this tends to be bitter. This dish may be prepared in advance and reheated slowly before serving. Do not add the yogurt until ready to serve.

Cook's Tip
If the yogurt is too thick to drizzle properly, thin with a little water or milk. Cook paprika and most spices briefly before adding any liquid to the recipe. This will develop the flavour and eliminate any harsh taste.

5

POULTRY DISHES

pages 160-195

SERVES 6-8

COUNTRY CHICKEN STEW

Peppers, potatoes, corn, tomatoes, onions and broad
beans are staple ingredients in this recipe.

1.5k/3lbs chicken portions
90g/6 tbsps flour
45g/3 tbsps butter or margarine
225g/8oz belly pork, rinded and cut into 5mm/¼ inch
    dice
3 medium onions, finely chopped
1.75l/3 pints water
3 400g/14oz cans tomatoes
45ml/3 tbsps tomato purée
120g/4oz fresh or frozen broad beans
120g/4oz sweetcorn
2 large red peppers, seeded and cut into small dice
3 medium potatoes, peeled and cut into 1.25cm/½ inch
    cubes
Salt and pepper
5-10ml/1-2 tsps cayenne pepper or tabasco, or to taste
10ml/2 tsps Worcester sauce
280ml/½ pint red wine

1. Shake the pieces of chicken in the flour in a plastic bag
as for Fried Chicken. In a large, deep sauté pan, melt the
butter until foaming. Place in the chicken without crowding
the pieces and brown over moderately high heat for about
10-12 minutes. Remove the chicken and set it aside.

2. In the same pan, fry the belly pork until the fat is rendered and the dice are crisp.

3. Add the onions and cook over moderate heat for about
10 minutes, or until softened but not browned.

4. Pour the water into a large stock pot or saucepan and
spoon in the onions, pork and any meat juices from the pan.
Add the chicken, tomatoes and tomato purée. Bring to the
boil, reduce the heat and simmer for about 1-1½ hours.

5. Add the broad beans, sweetcorn, peppers and
potatoes. Add cayenne pepper or tabasco to taste. Add the
Worcester sauce and red wine.

6. Cook for a further 30 minutes or until the chicken is
tender. Add salt and pepper to taste.

7. The stew should be rather thick, so if there is too much
liquid, remove the chicken and vegetables and boil down
the liquid to reduce it. If there is not enough liquid, add more
water or chicken stock.

Step 3 Add the onions and cook slowly until tender but not browned.

Step 4 Scrape the contents of the sauté pan into a large stock pot or saucepan of water.

Cook's Notes

Time
Preparation takes about 1 hour
and cooking takes about
2 hours.

Preparation
If desired, prepare the stew
ahead of time, leaving out the
last half hour of cooking. Bring slowly to
the boil and then simmer for about 30
minutes more before serving.

Freezing
The stew may be frozen for up
to 2 months in rigid
containers. Bring the stew to room
temperature before freezing.

SERVES 4-6

CHICKEN, SAUSAGE AND OKRA STEW

There is an exotic taste to this economical
chicken stew. The garlic sausage adds flavour instantly.

1.5kg/3lb chicken, cut into 6-8 pieces
120ml/4 fl oz oil
120g/4oz flour
1 large onion, finely chopped
1 large green pepper, roughly chopped
3 sticks celery, finely chopped
2 cloves garlic, crushed
225g/8oz garlic sausage, diced
1 litre/2 pints chicken stock
1 bay leaf
Dash tabasco
Salt and pepper
120g/4oz fresh okra
Cooked rice

1. Heat the oil in a large saut]e pan or frying pan and brown the chicken on both sides, 3-4 pieces at a time. Transfer the chicken to a plate and set it aside.

2. Lower the heat under the pan and add the flour. Cook over a very low heat for about 30 minutes, stirring constantly until the flour turns a rich, dark brown. Take the pan off the heat occasionally, so that the flour does not burn.

3. Add the onion, green pepper, celery, garlic and sausage to the pan and cook for about 5 minutes over very low heat, stirring continuously.

4. Pour on the stock and stir well. Add the bay leaf and a dash of tabasco, if desired, and return the chicken to the pan. Cover and cook for about 30 minutes or until the chicken is tender.

5. Top and tail the okra and cut each part into 2-3 pieces. If okra is small, leave whole. Add to the chicken and cook for a further 10-15 minutes. Remove the bay leaf and serve over rice.

Step 2 Continue cooking over low heat, stirring constantly as the flour begins to brown.

Step 3 When the flour is a rich dark brown, add the remaining sauce ingredients. Cook over a very low heat for 5 minutes, then add the stock slowly.

Cook's Notes

Time
Preparation takes about 30 minutes and cooking takes about 1 hour 25 minutes.

Cook's Tip
The oil and flour roux may be made ahead of time and kept in the refrigerator to use whenever needed. If the roux is cold, heat the liquid before adding.

Variation
May also be made with pork or turkey.

SERVES 6

TOMATO AND BACON FRIED CHICKEN

Not the usual crisp fried chicken, this is cooked
in a tomato sauce flavoured with garlic, herbs and wine.

1.5kg/3lb frying chicken, cut into serving pieces
Flour for dredging
Salt and pepper
90ml/6 tbsps oil
75g/5 tbsps butter or margarine
1 small onion, finely chopped
1 clove garlic, crushed
120g/4oz streaky bacon or green gammon, diced
6 tomatoes, peeled and chopped
10ml/2 tsps fresh thyme or 5ml/1 tsp dried thyme
Salt and pepper
140ml/¼ pint white wine
30ml/2 tbsps chopped parsley

1. Mix the flour with salt and pepper and dredge the
chicken lightly, shaking the pieces to remove any excess
flour. Heat the oil in a large sauté pan or frying pan and,
when hot, add the butter.

2. Add the chicken drumstick and thigh pieces skin side
down and allow to brown. Turn the pieces over and brown
on the other side. Brown over moderately low heat so that
the chicken cooks as well as browns. Push the chicken to
one side of the pan, add the breast meat, and brown in
the same way.

3. Add the garlic, onion and bacon or gammon to the pan
and lower the heat. Cook slowly for about 10 minutes, or
until the bacon browns slightly. Add the tomatoes and
thyme and lower the heat. Cook until the chicken is just
tender and the tomatoes are softened.

4. Using a draining spoon, transfer the chicken and other
ingredients to a serving dish and keep warm. Remove all
but about 60ml/4 tbsps of the fat from the pan and
deglaze with the wine, scraping up the browned bits from
the bottom. Bring to the boil and allow to reduce slightly.
Pour over the chicken to serve, and sprinkle with
chopped parsley.

Step 1 Dredge
the chicken very
lightly with flour
and shake to
remove the
excess.

Step 2 Brown all
the chicken on
both sides slowly,
until golden.

Cook's Notes

Preparation
Brown the chicken slowly so
that it cooks at the same time
as it browns. This will cut down on the
length of cooking time needed once all
the ingredients are added.

Time
Preparation takes about 25
minutes and cooking takes
about 30-40 minutes.

Variation
Add finely chopped green or
red pepper or celery along
with the onion and garlic. If more sauce
is desired, use one 400g/14 oz can of
tomatoes and juice. Substitute chicken
stock for the wine.

SERVES 4

PECAN CHICKEN

Pecans can be used in both
sweet and savoury dishes. Here, their rich,
sweet taste complements a stuffing for chicken.

4 boned chicken breasts
45g/3 tbsps butter or margarine
1 small onion, finely chopped
90g/3oz pork sausage meat
90g/3oz fresh breadcrumbs
5ml/1 tsp chopped thyme
5ml/1 tsp chopped parsley
1 small egg, lightly beaten
120g/4oz pecan halves
280ml/½ pint chicken stock
15ml/1 tbsp flour
30ml/2 tbsps sherry
Salt and pepper
Chopped parsley or 1 bunch watercress to garnish

1. Cut a small pocket in the thick side of each chicken breast using a small knife.

2. Melt 15g/1 tbsp butter in a small saucepan and add the onion. Cook a few minutes over gentle heat to soften. Add the sausage meat and turn up the heat to brown. Break up the sausage meat with a fork as it cooks.

3. Drain any excess fat and add the breadcrumbs, herbs and a pinch of salt and pepper. Allow to cool slightly and add enough egg to hold the mixture together. Chop pecans, reserving 8, and add to the stuffing.

4. Using a small teaspoon, fill the pocket in each chicken breast with some of the stuffing.

5. Melt 15g/1 tbsp butter in a casserole and place in the chicken breasts, skin side down first. Brown over moderate heat and turn over. Brown the other side quickly to seal.

6. Pour in the stock, cover the casserole and cook for about 25-30 minutes in a preheated 180°C/350°F/Gas Mark 4 oven until tender.

7. When chicken is cooked, remove it to a serving plate to keep warm. Reserve cooking liquid.

8. Melt remaining butter in a small saucepan and stir in the flour. Cook to a pale straw colour. Strain on the cooking liquid and add the sherry. Bring to the boil and stir constantly until thickened. Add the pecans and seasoning.

9. Spoon some of the sauce over the chicken. Garnish with chopped parsley or a bouquet of watercress.

Step 1 Use a small, sharp knife to cut a pocket in each chicken breast.

Step 4 Open each packet in the chicken and spoon in the stuffing.

Cook's Notes

Time
Preparation takes about 30 minutes and cooking takes about 40 minutes.

Variation
If pecans are unavailable, use hazelnuts. Crush the hazelnuts roughly for the garnish and brown lightly in the butter before adding flour for the sauce.

Serving Ideas
Serve with a rice or sauté potatoes.

SERVES 4-6

CHICKEN AND VEGETABLE STEW

A combination of chicken, broad beans, peppers
and onions made into an aromatic stew.

1.5kg/3lb chicken, cut in 8 pieces
90g/6 tbsps butter or margarine
45g/3 tbsps flour
1 large red pepper, diced
1 large green pepper, diced
6 spring onions, chopped
420ml/¾ pint chicken stock
180g/6oz broad beans
5ml/1 tsp chopped thyme
Salt, pepper and pinch nutmeg

1. To cut the chicken in 8 pieces, remove the legs first. Cut between the legs and the body of the chicken.

2. Bend the legs backwards to break the joint and cut away from the body.

3. Cut the drumstick and thigh joints in half.

4. Cut down the breastbone with a sharp knife and then use poultry shears to cut through the bone and ribcage to remove the breast joints from the back.

5. Cut both breast joints in half, leaving some white meat attached to the wing joint.

6. Heat the butter in a large sauté pan and when foaming add the chicken, skin side down. Brown on one side, turn over and brown other side. Remove the chicken and add the flour to the pan. Cook to a pale straw colour. Add the peppers and onions and cook briefly.

7. Pour on the chicken stock and bring to the boil. Stir constantly until thickened. Add the chicken, broad beans, thyme, seasoning and nutmeg. Cover the pan and cook about 25 minutes, or until the chicken is tender.

Step 2 Bend chicken legs back to break the joint, then cut between leg and body of chicken.

Step 4 Cut through the breastbone and rib cage with poultry shears.

Step 5 Cut the breast joint in two, leaving white meat attached to the wing.

Cook's Notes

Time
Preparation takes about 35 minutes and cooking takes about 40 minutes.

Preparation
For crisper vegetables, add them after the chicken and sauce have cooked for about 15 minutes.

SERVES 4

CHICKEN IN RED WINE

The perfect supper dish for guests,
family or friends. It's delicious and can
be prepared in advance.

225g/8oz thick cut streaky bacon
430ml/¾ pint water
30g/1oz butter or margarine
12-16 button onions
225g/8oz mushrooms, left whole if small, quartered if large
430ml/¾ pint dry red wine
1.5kg/3lb chicken, cut into eight pieces
1 bouquet garni
1 clove garlic, crushed
45g/3 tbsps flour
430ml/¾ pint chicken stock
30ml/2 tbsps chopped parsley
4 slices bread, crusts removed
Oil for frying
Salt and pepper

Step 1 Cut the bacon into small strips and blanch to remove excess salt.

1. Preheat oven to 180°C/350°F/Gas Mark 4. Cut the bacon into strips about 5mm/¼ inch thick. Bring water to the boil and blanch the bacon by simmering for 5 minutes. Remove the bacon with a draining spoon and dry on paper towels. Re-boil the water and drop in the onions. Allow them to boil rapidly for 2-3 minutes and then plunge into cold water and peel. Set the onions aside with the bacon.

2. Melt half the butter in a large frying pan over moderate heat and add the bacon and onions. Fry over high heat, stirring frequently and shaking the pan, until the bacon and onions are golden brown. Remove them with a draining spoon and leave on paper towels. Add the remaining butter to the saucepan and cook the mushrooms for 1-2 minutes. Remove them and set them aside with the onions and bacon.

3. Reheat the frying pan and brown the chicken, a few pieces at a time. When all the chicken is browned, transfer it to a large ovenproof casserole.

4. Pour the wine into a small saucepan and boil it to reduce to about 280ml/½ pint. Add the bouquet garni and garlic to the casserole.

5. Pour off all but 15ml/1 tbsp of fat from the frying pan and stir in the flour. Cook over gentle heat, scraping any of the browned chicken juices from the bottom of the pan. Pour in the reduced wine and add the stock. Bring the sauce to the boil over high heat, stirring constantly until thickened. Strain over the chicken in the casserole and cover tightly.

6. Place in the oven and cook for 20 minutes. After that time, add the bacon, onions and mushrooms and continue cooking for a further 15-20 minutes, or until the chicken is tender. Remove the bouquet garni and season with salt and pepper.

7. Cut each of the bread slices into 4 triangles. Heat enough oil in a large frying pan to cover the triangles of bread. When the oil is very hot, add the bread triangles two at a time and fry until golden brown and crisp. Drain on paper towels. To serve, arrange the chicken in a deep dish, pour over the sauce and vegetables and arrange the fried bread croûtes around the outside of the dish. Sprinkle with chopped parsley.

Cook's Notes

! Watchpoint
Make sure the oil for frying the croûtes is hot enough when the bread is added, otherwise croûtes can be very oily.

Cook's Tip
Blanching the bacon in boiling water removes excess saltiness. Boiling the onions makes them easier to peel.

Time
Preparation takes 30-40 minutes, cooking takes about 50 minutes.

SERVES 4-6

CHICKEN LIVER PILAFF

A mixture of finely chopped chicken
livers, celery, green pepper and
onions adds interest to rice.

225g/8oz long-grain rice
570ml/1 pint water
450g/1lb chicken livers
1 stick celery, roughly chopped
1 green pepper, seeded and roughly chopped
2 medium onions, roughly chopped
30ml/2 tbsps oil
Salt and pepper
Chopped parsley to garnish

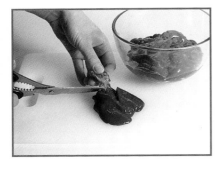

Step 2 Pick over
chicken livers to
remove fat and
any discoloured
portions.

1. Cook the rice in the water with a pinch of salt. When cooked, leave to stand while preparing the liver.

2. Pick over the chicken livers to remove any fat and discoloured portions.

3. Place the livers, celery, pepper and onions in a food processor and process to finely chop the ingredients. The mixture will look soupy.

4. Heat the oil in a large frying pan and add the liver mixture. Cook over moderate heat, stirring gently.

5. Once the mixture has set, turn down the heat to very low, cover the pan and cook about 30-40 minutes, or until rich golden brown in colour.

6. Stir in the cooked rice, fluffing up the mixture with a fork. Heat through, season to taste and serve garnished with chopped parsley.

Step 4 Cook the
liver mixture,
stirring gently, in
oil in a large
frying pan.

Step 6 When the
liver mixture has
browned, stir in
the cooked rice
using a fork to fluff
the mixture up.

Cook's Notes

Time
Preparation takes about 20 minutes and cooking takes about 30-40 minutes.

Serving Ideas
The rice may be served as a main dish, in which case this recipe serves 2-3. The rice is often served cold as a starter. Also use the recipe as a side dish.

Cook's Tip
Removing the yellowish or greenish portions from the chicken livers will eliminate bitter taste.

SERVES 4

PIGEONS IN WINE

Since pigeons often cost as little as 50p
each, you can make this dish inexpensively,
yet no one will ever guess.

4 pigeons
2.5ml/½ tsp each salt, pepper and paprika
30ml/2 tbsps oil
30g/2 tbsps butter or margarine
340g/12oz button onions
2 stick celery, sliced
4 carrots, peeled and sliced
60g/4 tbsps flour
430ml/¾ pint chicken stock
140ml/¼ pint dry red wine
120g/4oz button mushrooms, quartered or left whole if
    small
90g/3oz fresh or frozen broad beans
10ml/2 tsps tomato purée (optional)
30ml/2 tbsps chopped mixed herbs
Pinch salt

Step 1 Season the pigeons inside their cavities with the salt and spice mixture.

1. Wipe the pigeons with a damp cloth and season them inside the cavities with the salt, pepper and paprika.

2. Heat the oil in a heavy-based casserole and add the butter or margarine. Once it is foaming, place in the pigeons, two at a time if necessary, and brown them on all sides, turning them frequently. Remove from the casserole and set them aside.

3. To peel the button onions quickly, trim the root ends slightly and drop the onions into rapidly boiling water. Allow it to come back to the boil for about 1 minute. Transfer to cold water and leave to cool completely. The skins should come off easily. Trim roots completely.

4. Add the onions, celery and carrots to the fat in the casserole and cook for about 5 minutes to brown slightly. Add the flour and cook until golden brown, stirring constantly.

5. Pour in the stock and the wine and stir well. Bring to the boil over high heat until thickened.

6. Stir in the tomato purée, if using, and return the pigeons to the casserole along with any liquid that has accumulated. Partially cover the casserole and simmer gently for about 40-45 minutes, or until the pigeons are tender. Add the mushrooms and broad beans halfway through the cooking time. To serve, skim any excess fat from the surface of the sauce and sprinkle over the chopped parsley.

Cook's Notes

Time
Preparation takes about 30 minutes and cooking takes about 50 minutes-1 hour.

Variation
The casserole may be prepared with poussins, quail or pheasant. The quail will take only half the cooking time.

SERVES 4-6

CHICKEN WITH AUBERGINE AND HAM STUFFING

Aubergines and ham make an unusual stuffing
and add interest to roast chicken.

1.5kg/3lb roasting chicken
1 small aubergine
30g/2 tbsps butter or margarine
1 small onion, finely chopped
120g/4oz ham, chopped
120g/4oz fresh breadcrumbs
10ml/2 tsps chopped mixed herbs
Salt and pepper
1-2 eggs, beaten
30g/2 tbsps additional butter, softened

Step 1 Sprinkle the cut surface of the aubergine lightly with salt and leave to stand.

1. Cut the aubergine in half lengthways and remove stem. Lightly score the surface with a sharp knife and sprinkle with salt. Leave to stand for about 30 minutes for the salt to draw out any bitter juices.

2. Melt 30g/2 tbsps butter in a medium saucepan and when foaming, add the onion. Cook slowly to soften slightly.

3. Rinse the aubergine and pat dry. Cut into 1.25cm/½ inch cubes. Cook with the onion until fairly soft. Add the remaining stuffing ingredients, beating in the egg gradually until the mixture just holds together. Add salt and pepper to taste.

4. Remove the fat from just inside the chicken cavity. Fill the neck end with the stuffing. Place any extra in a greased casserole. Tuck the wing tips under the chicken to hold the neck flap down. Tie the legs together and place the chicken in a roasting pan. Spread over the remaining softened butter and roast in a pre-heated 180°C/350°F/Gas Mark 4 oven for about 1 hour, or until the juices from the chicken run clear when the thickest part of the thigh is pierced with a sharp knife. Cook extra stuffing, covered for the last 35 minutes of cooking time. Leave the chicken to stand for 10 minutes before carving. If desired, make a gravy with the pan juices.

Step 4 Remove the fat from just inside the cavity opening.

Cook's Notes

 Time
Preparation takes about 30 minutes and cooking takes about 5-6 minutes for the stuffing and about 1 hour for the chicken.

Variation
Other ingredients, such as chopped red or green peppers, celery or spring onions, may be added to the stuffing.

Watchpoint
Do not stuff the chicken until ready to cook.

SERVES 4-6

CHICKEN AND SAUSAGE RISOTTO

This is really a one pot meal and one you
won't have to cook in the oven.

1.5kg/3lbs chicken portions, skinned, boned, and cut
into cubes
45g/3 tbsps butter or margarine
1 large onion, roughly chopped
3 sticks celery, roughly chopped
1 large green pepper, seeded and roughly chopped
1 clove garlic, crushed
Salt and pepper
225g/8oz uncooked rice
400g/14oz canned tomatoes
180g/6oz smoked sausage, cut into 1.25cm/½ inch dice
850ml/1½ pints chicken stock
Chopped parsley

1. Use the chicken back skin, onion and celery trimming
to make stock. Cover the ingredients with water, bring to
the boil and then simmer slowly for 1 hour. Strain and
reserve.

2. Melt the butter or margarine in a large saucepan and
add the onion. Cook slowly to brown and then add the
celery, green pepper and garlic and cook briefly.

3. Add the salt and pepper and the rice, stirring to mix
well.

4. Add the chicken, tomatoes, sausage and stock and mix
well. Bring to the boil, then reduce the heat to simmering
and cook about 20-25 minutes, stirring occasionally until
the chicken is done and the rice is tender. The rice should
have absorbed most of the liquid by the time it has cooked.

Remove the skin
from the chicken
and set aside.

Step 1 Put the
skin and bones in
a large stock pot
with the onion and
celery trimmings
to make the stock.
Add water to
cover.

Cook's Notes

Time
Preparation takes about 35-40
minutes and cooking takes
about 20-25 minutes.

Preparation
Check the level of liquid
occasionally as the rice is
cooking and add more water or stock
as necessary. If there is a lot of liquid
left and the rice is nearly cooked,
uncover the pan and boil rapidly.

Serving Ideas
Add a green salad to make a
complete meal.

SERVES 4

POACHED CHICKEN WITH CREAM SAUCE

Plainly cooked chicken can be as flavourful
as it is attractive.

2kg/4½lb whole chicken
8-10 sticks celery, washed, cut into 7.5cm/3 inch lengths
   and tops reserved
120g/4oz streaky bacon, thickly sliced
2 cloves garlic, crushed
1 large onion, stuck with 4 cloves
1 bay leaf
1 sprig fresh thyme
Salt and pepper
Water to cover
90g/6 tbsps butter or margarine
90g/6 tbsps flour
280ml/½ pint single cream

1. Remove the fat from just inside the cavity of the chicken. Singe any pin feathers over gas flame or pull them out with tweezers.

2. Tie the chicken legs together and tuck the wing tips under to hold the neck flap. Place the chicken in a large casserole or stock pot. Chop the celery tops and add to the pot. Place the bacon over the chicken and add the garlic, onion with the cloves, bay leaf, sprig thyme, salt, pepper and water to cover.

3. Bring to the boil, reduce the heat and simmer gently, covered, for 50 minutes or until the chicken is just tender.

4. Cut the celery into 7.5cm/3 inch lengths and add to the chicken. Simmer a further 20 minutes, or until the celery is just tender.

5. Remove the chicken to a serving plate and keep warm. Strain the stock and reserve the bacon and celery pieces. Skim fat off the top of the stock and add enough water to make up 570ml/1 pint, if necessary.

6. Melt 15g/1 tbsp of the butter or margarine in the casserole and sauté the bacon until just crisp. Drain on paper towels and crumble roughly.

7. Melt the rest of the butter in the casserole or pan and when foaming take off the heat. Stir in the flour and gradually add the chicken stock. Add the cream and bring to the boil, stirring constantly. Simmer until the mixture is thickened.

8. Untie the legs and trim the leg ends. If desired, remove the skin from the chicken and coat with the sauce. Garnish with the bacon and the reserved celery pieces.

Step 2 Tie the legs together but do not cross them over. Tuck the neck skin under the wing tips.

Step 3 Arrange the bacon over the chicken, add the celery tops and the rest of the ingredients.

Cook's Notes

Time
Preparation takes about 25 minutes and cooking takes about 1 hour 10 minutes.

Serving Ideas
The chicken may be jointed into 8 pieces before coating with sauce, if desired. Cut the leg joints in two, dividing the thigh and the drumstick. Cut the breast in two, leaving some white meat attached to the wings. Cut through any bones with scissors.

Variation
Sliced or whole baby carrots may be added with the celery. Small onions may also be cooked with the celery and peeled in the same way as for the recipe for Creamed Onions.

SERVES 6

CHICKEN COBBLER

This dish is warming winter fare with
its creamy sauce and tender, light topping.

4 chicken joints, 2 breasts and 2 legs
1.5 litres/2½ pints water
1 bay leaf
4 whole peppercorns
2 carrots, peeled and diced
24 button onions, peeled
90g/6 tbsps frozen sweetcorn
140ml/¼ pint double cream
Salt

Cobbler Topping

400g/14oz plain flour
25ml/1½ tbsps baking powder
Pinch salt
75g/5 tbsps butter or margarine
340ml/12 fl oz milk
1 egg, beaten with a pinch of salt

1. Place the chicken in a deep saucepan with water, bay leaf and peppercorns. Cover and bring to the boil. Reduce the heat and allow to simmer for 20-30 minutes, or until the chicken is tender. Remove the chicken from the pot and allow to cool. Skim and discard the fat from the surface of the stock. Skin the chicken and remove the meat from the bones.

2. Continue to simmer the stock until reduced by about half. Strain the stock and add the carrots and onions. Cook until tender and add the sweetcorn. Stir in the cream and add the chicken. Pour into a casserole or into individual baking dishes.

3. To prepare the topping, sift the dry ingredients into a bowl or place them in a food processor and process once or twice to sift.

4. Rub in the butter or margarine until the mixture resembles small peas. Stir in enough of the milk until the mixture comes together.

5. Turn out onto a floured surface and knead lightly. Roll out with a floured rolling pin and cut with a pastry cutter. Brush the surface of each round with a mixture of egg and salt. Place the rounds on top of the chicken mixture and bake for 10-15 minutes in a pre-heated oven at 190°C/375°F/Gas Mark 5. Serve immediately.

Step 4 Rub the butter or margarine into the dry ingredients until the mixture resembles small peas.

Step 5 Roll out the mixture on a floured surface, cut into rounds and place on top of the chicken mixture.

Cook's Notes

Time
Preparation takes about 25 minutes and cooking takes about 20-30 minutes for the chicken, about 20 minutes to prepare the sauce, and about 10-15 minutes to finish off the dish.

Preparation
Once the topping has been prepared it must be baked immediately or the baking powder will stop working and the cobbler topping will not rise.

Variations
Diced potatoes and pimento may be added to the sauce along with other vegetables. Add chopped fresh parsley or a pinch of dried thyme as well, if desired.

SERVES 10-12

ROAST TURKEY WITH SAUSAGE STUFFING

1 fresh turkey weighing about 20lbs
90g/6 tbsps butter

Sausage Stuffing

60ml/4 tbsps oil
120g/4oz sausage meat
3 sticks celery, diced
2 onions, diced
120g/4oz chopped walnuts or pecans
120g/4oz raisins
450g/1lb day-old bread, made into small cubes
280ml/½ pint chicken stock
1.25ml/¼ tsp each dried thyme and sage
30g/2 tbsps chopped fresh parsley
Salt and pepper

1. Singe any pin feathers on the turkey by holding the bird over a gas flame. Alternatively, pull out the feathers with tweezers.

2. Remove the fat which is just inside the cavity of the bird.

3. To prepare the stuffing, heat the oil and cook the sausage meat, breaking it up with a fork as it cooks. Add the celery, onion, nuts and raisins and cook for about 5 minutes, stirring constantly.

4. Drain away the fat and add the herbs, cubes of bread and stock, and mix well. Season to taste.

5. Stuff the neck cavity of the bird, packing in as much stuffing as possible. Place remaining stuffing in an oiled casserole dish.

6. Tie the legs together but do not cross them over. Tuck the neck skin under the wing tips and, if desired, use a trussing needle and fine string to secure them.

7. Place the turkey on a rack, breast side up, in a roasting pan. Soften the butter and spread some over the breast and the legs. Place the turkey in a pre-heated 170°C/325°F/Gas Mark 3 oven and cover loosely with foil. Roast for about 2 hours, basting often. Cover the casserole and cook remaining stuffing during the last 45 minutes of the turkeys cooking time.

8. Remove the foil and continue roasting for another 2-2½ hours, or until the internal temperature in the thickest part of the thigh registers 180°C/350°F. Alternatively, pierce the thigh with a skewer – if the juices run clear then the turkey is done. Allow to rest for about 15-20 minutes before carving. Make gravy with the pan juices if desired and serve.

Step 8 Pierce the thigh with a skewer. The turkey is done when the juices run clear.

Cook's Notes

 Variation
Many different ingredients can be included in a turkey stuffing. Ham or crisply cooked bacon can be substituted for the sausage. A mixture of dried fruit may be used instead of all raisins. Chopped apple may also be included.

 Time
Preparation takes about 25-30 minutes and cooking takes about 4-4½hours.

 Cook's Tip
Leaving a turkey or other roast bird to stand for 15-20 minutes before carving keeps the natural juices in the meat.

 Watch Point
The stuffing may be prepared in advance, but do not stuff the bird until ready to roast. There is a danger of food poisoning if a turkey or any other bird is stuffed too long before cooking.

SERVES 6

SPICY SPANISH CHICKEN

Chilli peppers, coriander and sunny tomatoes
add warm Spanish flavour to grilled chicken.

6 boned chicken breasts
Grated rind and juice of 1 lime
30ml/2 tbsps olive oil
Coarsely ground black pepper
90ml/6 tbsps whole grain mustard
10ml/2 tsps paprika
4 ripe tomatoes, peeled, seeded and quartered
2 shallots, chopped
1 clove garlic, crushed
½ Jalapeno pepper or other chilli, seeded and chopped
5ml/1 tsp wine vinegar
Pinch salt
30ml/2 tbsps chopped fresh coriander
Whole coriander leaves to garnish

Step 1 Marinate chicken in a shallow dish, turning occasionally to coat.

1. Place chicken breasts in a shallow dish with the lime rind and juice, oil, pepper, mustard and paprika. Marinate for about 1 hour, turning occasionally.

2. To peel tomatoes easily, drop them into boiling water for about 5 seconds or less depending on ripeness. Place immediately in cold water. Peels should come off easily.

Step 2 Tomatoes peel easily when placed first in boiling water and then in cold.

3. Place tomatoes, shallots, garlic, chilli pepper, vinegar and salt in a food processor or blender and process until coarsely chopped. Stir in the cilantro by hand.

4. Place chicken on a grill pan and reserve the marinade. Cook chicken skin side uppermost for about 7-10 minutes, depending on how close the chicken is to the heat source. Baste frequently with the remaining marinade. Grill other side in the same way. Sprinkle with salt after grilling.

Step 4 Grill skin side of chicken until brown and crisp before turning pieces over.

5. Place chicken on serving plates and garnish top with cilantro (coriander) leaves or sprigs. Serve with a spoonful of the tomato relish on one side.

Cook's Notes

Time
Preparation takes about 1 hour and cooking takes 14-20 minutes.

Preparation
Tomato relish can be prepared in advance and kept in the refrigerator. It can also be served with other poultry, meat or seafood. It also makes a good dip for vegetable crudités or tortilla chips.

Watchpoint
When preparing chilli peppers, wear rubber gloves or at least be sure to wash hands thoroughly after handling them. Do not touch eyes or face before washing hands.

SERVES 6

CHICKEN WITH CHERRIES

Canned cherries make an easy sauce
that really dresses up chicken.

6 chicken breasts, skinned and boned
Oil
1 sprig fresh rosemary
Grated rind and juice of half a lemon
450g/1lb canned black cherries, pitted
Salt and pepper
10ml/2 tsps cornflour

Step 1 Cook the chicken breasts until just lightly browned. Watch carefully, as skinned chicken will dry out easily.

1. Heat about 60ml/4 tbsps oil in a sauté pan over moderate heat. Place in the chicken breasts, skinned side down first. Cook until just lightly browned. Turn over and cook the second side about 2 minutes.

2. Remove any oil remaining in the pan and add the rosemary, lemon rind, wine and salt and pepper. Bring to the boil and then lower the heat.

3. Add the cherries and their juice. Cook, covered, 15 minutes or until the chicken is tender. Remove the chicken and cherries and keep them warm. Discard rosemary.

4. Mix the cornflour and lemon juice. Add several spoonfuls of the hot sauce to the cornflour mixture. Return the mixture to the sauté pan and bring to the boil, stirring constantly, until thickened and cleared.

5. Pour sauce over the chicken and cherries. Heat through and serve.

Cook's Notes

Time
Preparation takes about 20 minutes if using pre-skinned and boned chicken breasts. Allow an extra 15 minutes to bone the chicken yourself.

Preparation
Serve the chicken dish on the day that it is cooked – it does not keep well.

Serving Ideas
Serve with plain boiled rice or Wild Rice Pilaff. Accompany with a green vegetable such as lightly steamed mangetout.

SERVES 4

FRIED CHICKEN

Fried Chicken is easy to do and
when it's home made, it's much
better than a take away!

1.5k/3lb chicken portions
2 eggs
225g/8oz flour
5ml/1 tsp each salt, paprika and sage
2.5ml/½ tsp black pepper
Pinch cayenne pepper (optional)
Oil for frying
Parsley or watercress

Step 4 Coat the chicken on all sides with flour, shaking off the excess

Step 2 Dip the chicken pieces in the egg to coat them well.

Step 6 Fry the chicken skin side first for 12 minutes, turn over and fry a further 12 minutes.

1. Rinse chicken and pat dry.

2. Beat the eggs in a large bowl and add the chicken one piece at a time, turning to coat.

3. Mix flour and seasonings in a large paper or plastic bag.

4. Place chicken pieces coated with egg into the bag one at a time, close bag tightly and shake to coat each piece of chicken. Alternatively, dip each coated chicken piece in a bowl of seasoned flour, shaking off the excess.

5. Heat oil in a large frying pan to the depth of about 1.25cm/½ inch.

6. When the oil is hot, add the chicken skin side down first. Fry about 12 minutes and then turn over. Fry a further 12 minutes or until the juices run clear.

7. Drain the chicken on paper towels and serve immediately. Garnish serving plate with parsley or watercress.

Cook's Notes

 Time
Preparation takes about 20 minutes and cooking takes about 24 minutes.

Preparation
The chicken should not be crowded in the frying pan. If your pan is small, fry the chicken in several batches.

 Cook's Tip
When coating anything for frying, be sure to coat it just before cooking. If left to stand, coating will usually become very soggy.

SERVES 6

COUNTRY CAPTAIN CHICKEN

A flavourful dish named for
a sea captain with a taste for
the spicy cuisine of India.

1.5kg/3lbs chicken portions
Seasoned flour
90ml/6 tbsps oil
1 medium onion, chopped
1 medium green pepper, seeded and chopped
1 clove garlic, crushed
Pinch salt and pepper
10ml/2 tsps curry powder
2 400g/14oz cans tomatoes
10ml/2 tsps chopped parsley
5ml/1 tsp chopped marjoram
60ml/4 tbsps currants or raisins
120g/4oz blanched almond halves

1. Remove skin from the chicken and dredge with flour, shaking off the excess.

2. Heat the oil and brown the chicken on all sides until golden. Remove to an ovenproof casserole.

3. Pour off all but 30ml/2 tbsps of the oil. Add the onion, pepper and garlic and cook slowly to soften.

4. Add the seasonings and curry powder and cook, stirring frequently, for 2 minutes. Add the tomatoes, parsley, marjoram and bring to the boil. Pour the sauce over the chicken, cover and cook in a pre-heated 180°C/350°F Gas Mark 4 oven for 45 minutes. Add the currants or raisins during the last 15 minutes.

5. Meanwhile, toast the almonds in the oven on a baking sheet along with the chicken. Stir them frequently and watch carefully. Sprinkle over the chicken just before serving.

Step 4 Add the curry powder to the vegetables in the frying pan and cook for two minutes over low heat stirring frequently.

Step 4 Cook the remaining sauce ingredients and pour over the chicken.

Step 5 Toast the almonds on a baking sheet in the oven until light golden brown.

Cook's Notes

Time
Preparation takes about 30 minutes and cooking takes about 50 minutes.

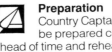

Preparation
Country Captain Chicken can be prepared completely ahead of time and reheated for about 20 minutes in a moderate oven.

Serving Ideas
If desired, serve the chicken with an accompaniment of rice

SERVES 4

CHICKEN WITH RED PEPPERS

Easy as this recipe is, it looks and tastes good
enough for guests.

4 large red peppers
4 skinned and boned chicken breasts
25ml/1½ tbsps oil
Salt and pepper
1 clove garlic, finely chopped
45ml/3 tbsps white wine vinegar
2 spring onions, finely chopped
Sage leaves for garnish

Step 1 Flatten the peppers with the palm of the hand and brush them with oil.

1. Cut the peppers in half and remove the stems, cores and seeds. Flatten the peppers with the palm of your hand and brush the skin sides lightly with oil.

2. Place the peppers skin side up on the rack of a pre-heated grill and cook about 5cm/2 inches away from the heat source until the skins are well blistered and charred.

3. Wrap the peppers in a clean towel and allow them to stand until cool. Peel off the skins with a small vegetable knife. Cut into thin strips and set aside.

4. Place the chicken breasts between two sheets of dampened greaseproof paper and flatten by hitting with a rolling pin or meat mallet.

5. Heat 25ml/1½ tbsps oil in a large frying pan. Season the chicken breasts on both sides and place in the hot oil. Cook 5 minutes, turn over and cook until tender and lightly browned. Remove the chicken and keep it warm.

6. Add the pepper strips, garlic, vinegar and spring onions to the pan and cook briefly until the vinegar loses its strong aroma.

7. Place the chicken breasts on serving plates. Spoon over the pan juices.

8. Arrange the pepper mixture with the chicken and garnish with the sage leaves.

Step 2 Cook the peppers until the skins are blistered and well charred.

Step 3 Peel off the skins using a small vegetable knife.

Cook's Notes

Time
Preparation takes about 35-40 minutes and cooking takes about 10 minutes to char the peppers and about 20 minutes to finish the dish.

Variation
For convenience, the dish may be prepared with canned pimento caps instead of red peppers. These will be softer so cook the garlic, vinegar and onions to soften, and then add pimento.

Buying Guide
If fresh sage is unavailable, substitute coriander or parsley leaves as a garnish.

6

SALADS

SERVES 4

TOMATO AND ORANGE SALAD WITH MOZZARELLA AND BASIL

Tomatoes and mozzarella cheese are a common salad combination.
The addition of oranges makes this just a little bit different.

4 large tomatoes
4 small oranges
225g/8oz mozzarella cheese
8 fresh basil leaves
60ml/4 tbsps olive oil
15ml/1 tbsp white wine vinegar
Salt and pepper

Step 2 Peel the oranges in thin strips to help preserve the round shape of the fruit.

1. Remove the cores from the tomatoes and slice into rounds about 5mm/¼ inch thick.

2. Cut the slice from the top and bottom of each orange and, using a serrated fruit knife, remove the peel in thin strips. Make sure to cut off all the white pith. Slices oranges into 5mm/¼ inch thick rounds. Slice the mozzarella cheese into the same thickness.

3. Arrange the tomatoes, oranges and mozzarella in overlapping circles, alternating each ingredient.

4. Use scissors to shred the basil leaves finely, and sprinkle over the salad.

5. Mix the remaining ingredients together well and spoon over the salad. Chill briefly before serving.

Step 3 Arrange the ingredients in overlapping circles.

Step 4 Use scissors to finely shred the basil leaves over the top of the salad.

Cook's Notes

Time
Preparation takes about 20-25 minutes.

Preparation
Shred the basil leaves just before serving, since they tend to turn black if cut and left to stand.

Buying Guide
Fresh basil is available in produce sections of most large supermarkets almost all year long.

SERVES 4-6

MUSHROOM SALAD

Use ordinary button mushrooms or a more
exotic variety. Which ever you choose this
salad is easy to prepare.

450g/1lb mushrooms
1 medium onion
45ml/3 tbsps oil
15ml/1 tbsp chopped parsley
1 dill cucumber, diced
3-4 tomatoes, peeled, seeded and diced
60ml/4 tbsps oil
15ml/1 tbsp wine vinegar
Salt and pepper
Pinch sugar

1. Slice the mushrooms thinly and chop the onion finely.
Heat 45ml/3 tbsps oil in a large sauté pan and add the
mushrooms and onions. Cook for about 2-3 minutes to
soften slightly. Remove from the heat and allow to cool.

2. When the mushrooms and onions have completely
cooled, add the parsley, dill cucumber and tomatoes. Mix
together the oil and vinegar, sugar and salt and pepper and
pour over the other ingredients. Stir gently to coat evenly
and allow to stand for 1-2 hours in the refrigerator before
serving.

To make tomatoes
easier to peel, first
drop them into
boiling water.

Use a small,
sharp knife to
remove the peel.

Cook's Notes

 Serving Ideas
To serve as a first course,
spoon the mushroom salad
on top of curly endive or finely
shredded lettuce. Serve with melba
toast, brown bread and butter or rolls.

 Variation
If desired, leave out the dill
cucumber. Substitute spring
onions and add them at the end before
refrigerating the salad.

Cook's Tip
The salad may be prepared a
day in advance. Add the
tomatoes 1 hour before serving.

SERVES 6

PEANUT COLESLAW

This lively sweet-sour dressing, along
with roasted peanuts gives a whole
new taste to basic coleslaw.

1 small head white cabbage, finely shredded
2 carrots, shredded
10ml/2 tsps celery seed
120g/4oz dry-roasted peanuts
1 egg
140ml/¼ pint white wine vinegar
140ml/¼ pint water
2.5ml/½ tsp dry mustard
30ml/2 tbsps sugar

1. Combine the vegetables, celery seed and peanuts in a
large bowl.

2. Beat the egg in a small bowl.

3. Add vinegar, water, mustard and sugar and blend
thoroughly.

4. Place the bowl in a pan of very hot water and whisk until
thickened. Cool and pour over the vegetables.

Step 3 Add the
vinegar, water,
mustard and
sugar to the egg
and blend
thoroughly.

Step 4 Place in a
pan of very hot
water and whisk
until thickened.

Cook's Notes

Time
Preparation takes about 30
minutes.

Variation
Shredded red cabbage and
finely chopped onion may be
added to the salad, if desired.

Preparation
The salad may be prepared
ahead of time and kept in the
refrigerator overnight.

SERVES 4

DRESSED CRAB SALAD

The rosy hued dressing is both creamy and
piquant – perfect for crab meat.

2 large cooked crabs
1 head iceberg lettuce
4 large tomatoes
4 hard-boiled eggs
16 black olives
280ml/½ pint prepared mayonnaise
60ml/4 tbsps whipping cream
60ml/4 tbsps chilli sauce or tomato chutney
½ green pepper, seeded and finely diced
3 spring onions, finely chopped
Salt and pepper

Step 1 Turn crabs over and press up with thumbs to separate the under-body from the shell.

1. To prepare the crabs, break off the claws and set them aside. Turn the crabs over and press up with thumbs to separate the body from the shell of each.

2. Cut the body into quarters and use a skewer to pick out the white meat. Discard the stomach sac and the lungs (dead-man's fingers). Scrape out the brown meat from the shell to use, if desired.

3. Crack the large claws and legs and remove the meat. Break into shreds, discarding any shell or cartilage. Combine all the meat and set it aside.

4. Shred the lettuce finely, quarter the tomatoes and chop the eggs.

5. Combine the mayonnaise, cream, chilli sauce or chutney, green pepper and spring onions and mix well.

6. Arrange the shredded lettuce on serving plates and divide the crab meat evenly.

7. Spoon some of the dressing over each serving of crab and sprinkle with the chopped egg. Garnish each serving with tomato wedges and olives and serve the remaining dressings separately.

Cook's Notes

Time
Preparation takes about 30-40 minutes.

Preparation
To shred lettuce finely, break off the leaves and stack them up a few at a time. Use a large, sharp knife to cut across the leaves into thin shreds.

Variation
Frozen crab meat may be used instead of fresh. Make sure it is completely defrosted and well drained before using. Pick through the meat to remove any bits of shell or cartilage left behind.

SERVES 6

CRUNCHY CABBAGE SALAD

Walnuts and avocado add interest to a
colourful variation on coleslaw.

1 small head red cabbage
1 avocado, peeled and cubed
1 carrot, grated
4 spring onions, shredded
120g/4oz chopped walnuts
90ml/6 tbsps oil
30ml/2 tbsps white wine vinegar
10ml/2 tsps dry mustard
Salt and pepper

1. Cut the cabbage in quarters and remove the core. Use a large knife to shred finely or use the thick slicing blade on a food processor.

2. Prepare the avocado as for Avocado Soup and cut it into small cubes.

3. Combine the cabbage, avocado and shredded carrot with the onions and walnuts in a large bowl.

4. Mix the remaining ingredients together well and pour over the salad. Toss carefully to avoid breaking up the avocado. Chill before serving.

Step 1 Remove the core from the cabbage quarters and shred with a sharp knife or use a food processor.

Step 4 Mixing the salad with your hands prevents the avocado from breaking up too much.

Cook's Notes

Time
Preparation takes about 25-30 minutes.

Serving Ideas
Serve as a side dish with chicken or as part of a salad buffet.

Preparation
The salad may be prepared a day in advance and the avocado and dressing added just before serving.

SERVES 4-6

PRAWN AND PINEAPPLE SALAD

Serve as a starter or main summer dish. Either way
the combination of flavours is superb!

450g/1lb cooked, peeled prawns
450g/1lb seedless white grapes, halved if large
6 sticks celery, thinly sliced on diagonal
120g/4oz toasted flaked almonds
120g/4oz canned water chestnuts, sliced or diced
225g/8oz canned lychees or 340g/12oz fresh lychees,
  peeled
1 small fresh pineapple, peeled, cored and cut into
  pieces
430ml/¾ pint mayonnaise
15ml/1 tbsp honey
15ml/1 tbsp light soy sauce
30ml/2 tbps mild curry powder
Juice of half a lime
Chinese leaves or Belgian endive (chicory)

1. Combine the prawns, grapes, celery, almonds, water
chestnuts and lychees in a large bowl. Trim off the top and
bottom of the pineapple and quarter. Slice off the points of
each quarter to remove the core.

2. Slice the pineapple skin away and cut the flesh into bite-
size pieces. Add to the prawns and toss to mix.

3. Break the Chinese leaves or endive and wash them
well. If using Chinese leaves, shred the leafy part finely,
saving the thicker ends of the leaves for other use. Place the
Chinese leaves on salad plates. Mix the remaining dressing
ingredients thoroughly. Pile the salad ingredients onto the
leaves and spoon over some of the dressing, leaving the
ingredients showing. Separate chicory leaves and arrange
them whole. Serve remaining dressing separately.

Step 1 Trim the
point of each
quarter of
pineapple to
remove the core.

Step 2 Use a
serrated fruit knife
to slice between
the skin and
pineapple flesh.

Step 2 Add
pineapple pieces
to the prawns and
mix well.

Cook's Notes

Time
Preparation takes about 30
minutes.

Serving Ideas
Serve as a main course salad
for lunch or a light dinner.
Serve in smaller quantities as a starter.

Variation
Other seafood may be
substituted for the prawns.
Crab sticks will be less expensive than
dressed crab.

SERVES 4

CHICKEN AND AVOCADO SALAD

The creamy herb dressing complements
this easy summer salad.

8 anchovy fillets, soaked in milk, rinsed and dried
1 spring onion, chopped
30g/2 tbsps chopped fresh tarragon
45g/3 tbsps chopped chives
60g/4 tbsps chopped parsley
280ml/½ pint prepared mayonnaise
140ml/¼ pint natural yogurt
30ml/2 tbsps tarragon vinegar
Pinch sugar and cayenne pepper
1 large head lettuce
450g/1lb cooked chicken
1 avocado, peeled and sliced or cubed
15ml/1 tbsp lemon juice

1. Combine all the ingredients, except the lettuce, avocado and chicken in a food processor. Work the ingredients until smooth, and well mixed. Leave in the refrigerator at least 1 hour for the flavours to blend.

2. Shred the lettuce or tear into bite-size pieces and arrange on plates.

3. Top the lettuce with the cooked chicken cut into strips or cubes.

4. Spoon the dressing over the chicken. Brush the avocado slices or toss the cubes with lemon juice and garnish the salad. Serve any remaining dressing separately.

Step 1 The dressing should be very well blended after working in a food processor. Alternatively, use a hand blender.

Step 3 Arrange lettuce on individual plates and top with shredded chicken.

Cook's Notes

Time
Preparation takes about 30 minutes.

Preparation
Dressing may be prepared ahead of time and kept in the refrigerator for a day or two.

Serving Ideas
The dressing may be served as a dip for vegetable cruditïs or with a tossed salad.

SERVES 4-6

CAESAR SALAD

A classic salad from the United States,
said to have been concocted one evening
from the only ingredients left in the kitchen.

6 anchovy fillets, soaked in 60ml/4 tbsps milk
280ml/½ pint olive oil
1 clove garlic, left whole
4 slices French bread, cut into 1.25cm/½" cubes
1 egg, cooked 1 minute
1 head Cos lettuce
Juice of 1 small lemon
Salt and pepper
60g/4 tbsps grated Parmesan cheese

Step 2 Fry the cubes of French bread in the hot oil, stirring them constantly for even browning.

1. Leave the anchovies to soak in the milk for 15 minutes. Rinse and pat dry on paper towels. Chop roughly.

2. Crush the garlic and leave in the oil for about 30 minutes. Heat all but 90ml/6 tbsps of the oil in a frying pan until hot. Fry the cubes of bread until golden brown, stirring constantly with a metal spoon for even browning. Drain on paper towels.

3. Break the cooked egg into a bowl and beat well with the lemon juice, salt and pepper. Toss the lettuce with the remaining garlic oil and anchovies. Add the egg mixture and toss to coat well. Place in a clean serving bowl and sprinkle over the croûtons and Parmesan cheese. Serve at room temperature.

Step 3 To make the dressing, break the egg into the bowl and mix well with the lemon juice and seasoning until slightly thickened.

Step 3 Add the oil to the lettuce separately and then toss with the egg dressing mixture.

Cook's Notes

Time
Preparation takes about 30 minutes and cooking takes about 3-5 minutes for the croûtons.

Cook's Tip
Soaking anchovy fillets in milk before using them neutralises the strong salty taste.

Watchpoint
Remove the croûtons from the hot fat when just barely brown enough. They continue to cook slightly in their own heat as they drain.

SERVES 4-6

SPICY EGG SALAD

Serve this as a starter or a main course.
If desired, substitute more
vegetables for the prawns.

4 eggs
Half a bunch of spring onions, chopped
Half a small red pepper, chopped
Half a small green pepper, chopped
120g/4oz cooked, peeled prawns
1 small jar artichoke hearts, drained and quartered

Dressing

90ml/6 tbsps oil
30ml/2 tbsps white wine vinegar
1 clove garlic, finely chopped
5ml/1 tsp dry mustard
2.5ml/½ tsp hot red pepper flakes
Salt

1. Prick the large end of the eggs with an egg pricker or a needle.

2. Lower each egg carefully into boiling, salted water. Bring the water back to the boil, rolling the eggs in the water with the bowl of a spoon.

3. Cook the eggs for 9 minutes once the water comes back to the boil. Drain and rinse under cold water until completely cool. Peel and quarter. Combine the eggs with the other ingredients in a large bowl.

4. Mix the dressing ingredients together using a whisk to get a thick emulsion.

5. Pour the dressing over the salad and mix carefully so that the eggs do not break up.

6. Serve on beds of shredded lettuce, if desired.

Step 2 Lower each egg carefully into the water and roll around with the bowl of a spoon to set the yolk.

Step 4 Mix the dressing ingredients together using a whisk to get a thick emulsion.

Cook's Notes

Time
Preparation takes about 25 minutes and cooking takes about 9 minutes to boil the eggs.

Preparation
If preparing the eggs in advance, leave in the shells and in cold water. This will prevent a grey ring forming around the yolks.

Cook's Tip
Rolling the eggs around in the hot water helps to set the yolk in the centre of the white and makes sliced or quartered eggs more attractive.

SERVES 6

SPRING SALAD

Don't save this salad just for spring – the ingredients are available all year round. Try it as a spread for sandwiches or a topping for canapes, too.

340-400g/12-14oz cottage cheese
1 carrot, coarsely grated
8 radishes, coarsely grated
2 spring onions, thinly sliced
Pinch salt and pepper
5ml/1 tsp chopped fresh dill or marjoram
140ml/¼ pint sour cream or thick yogurt
Lettuce leaves (red oak leaf lettuce, curly endive or radicchio)

1. If cottage cheese is very liquidy, pour into a fine strainer and leave to stand for about 15-20 minutes for some of the liquid to drain away. Alternatively, cut down on the amount of sour cream.

2. Peel the carrots and shred them using the coarse side of the grater or the coarse shredding blade in a food processor. Make sure the carrots are shredded into short strips.

Step 2 Using the coarse side of a grater, grate the carrots into short strips.

Step 3 Trim the root ends from the spring onions and any part of the green tops that look damaged.

Step 3 Use a large, sharp knife to slice through both onions at once to save time.

3. Shred the radishes with the grater and cut the onion into thin rounds with a large, sharp knife.

4. Mix all the ingredients together, except the lettuce leaves, and chill for about 20 minutes to blend all the flavours.

5. To serve, place lettuce leaves on individual plates and mound the cottage cheese salad mixture on top. If desired, sprinkle with more chopped fresh dill.

Cook's Notes

Variation
Add finely chopped red or green pepper or cucumber to the salad. If using cucumber, grate and sprinkle with salt. Leave to stand 30 minutes, rinse and pat dry.

Serving Ideas
Serve with thinly sliced wholemeal or rye bread, lightly buttered. The salad may also be served with French bread.

Time
Preparation takes about 20 minutes and salad requires 15-20 minutes refrigeration.

SERVES 6

SAUSAGE, APPLE & PEPPER KEBABS

Perfect for summer barbecues, these
are different, easy and inexpensive.

140ml/¼ pint honey (set)
5ml/1 tsp chopped fresh dill
120ml/4 fl oz white wine vinegar
450g/1lb ham sausage, cut in 5cm/2 inch pieces
2 large cooking apples, cored but not peeled
1 large red pepper, cored, seeded and cut into
    5cm/2 inch pieces

Step 3 Quarter
and core the
apple, but do not
peel. Cut length-
ways or crosswise
into small pieces.

Step 1 Mix the
honey and herbs
together and
gradually beat in
the vinegar.

Step 4 Cut
peppers in half
and remove the
core and seeds.
Also cut out any
white pith as this
tends to be bitter.

1. Mix together the honey and the herbs. Gradually whisk
in the vinegar to blend thoroughly.

2. Cut the sausage and place in the marinade, stirring to
coat evenly. Allow to marinate for about 2 hours.

3. Cut the apple in quarters and remove the cores. Cut in
half again crossways or lengthways as desired.

4. Cut the pepper in half and remove the core and seeds
and any white pith inside. Rinse under cold running water to

remove all the seeds. Cut the pepper into pieces about the
same size as the sausage and apple. Thread the ingredients onto skewers, alternating the pepper, sausage and
apple. Brush with the marinate and place under a pre-
heated grill. Cook for about 5-6 minutes, turning 2 or 3 times
and brushing frequently with the marinade. Pour over any
additional marinade to serve.

Cook's Notes

 Time
The sausage needs about 2
hours to marinate. Preparation
will take about 15 minutes, cooking
takes about 5-6 minutes.

Preparation
The kebabs may be cooked
over an outdoor barbecue
grill, as well.

 Variation
Other types of sausage, such
as smoked or garlic sausage,
may be used.

Serving Ideas
Serve on a bed of rice and
accompany with a green
salad.

Cook's Tip
For extra flavour, the apples
may also be mixed in with the
marinade. The vinegar will keep them
from going brown.

SERVES 4-6

MEAT SALAD

A salad made with cooked meat is an
ideal way to use up leftovers. You
can even use it as a starter.

450g/1lb diced cooked beef, veal, ham or tongue
2 dill cucumbers
1 medium onion
15ml/1 tbsp capers
15ml/1 tbsp chopped parsley
5m/1 tsp mustard
1 medium boiled potato, peeled and diced
Salt and pepper
1 hard-boiled egg

Dressing
30ml/2 tbsps olive oil
45ml/3 tbsps wine vinegar
45ml/3 tbsps cold beef stock

2. Combine the dressing ingredients and whisk well. Pour over the salad and toss gently to coat all the ingredients thoroughly. Chill for 2 hours before serving.

3. To slice the egg evenly, use an egg slicer. Peel the egg, place it in the slicer and pull down the wire cutter. Carefully remove the slices and use the best looking ones to garnish the top of the salad. Further slices may be combined with the rest of the ingredients.

Step 1 Using a large, sharp knife, cut crosswise into thin slices. If desired, the slices may be cut in half again so they are not so long.

Step 1 To slice an onion, peel and cut in half through the root end. Place flat side down on a cutting board.

Step 3 Use a wire egg slicer to make uniform slices of egg. Once the egg is sliced through, turn the egg slicer carefully over into the palm of your hand and gently extract the egg slices.

1. Cut the dill cucumbers into thin slices and combine with the meat in a large bowl. Slice the onion thinly and add it to the bowl. Add the remaining salad ingredients except the eggs.

Cook's Notes

Time
Preparation takes about 20 minutes with 2 hours to chill.

Variation
Use a combination of 3 or 4 different meats. Cooked or smoked sausage may also be used.

7

VEGETABLE
&
SIDE DISHES

pages 224-271

SERVES 6

STIR FRIED VEGETABLES WITH HERBS

Crisply cooked vegetables with plenty of chives
make a perfect side dish, hot or cold.

4 sticks celery
4 medium courgettes
2 red peppers, seeded
30-45ml/3-4 tbsps oil
Pinch salt and pepper
5ml/1 tsp chopped fresh oregano or marjoram
60ml/4 tbsps snipped fresh chives

Step 1 Cut the celery sticks into 1.25cm/½ inch slices using a large, sharp knife.

1. Slice the celery on the diagonal into pieces about 1.25cm/1½ inch thick.

2. Cut the courgettes in half lengthways and then cut into 1.25cm/½ inch thick slices.

3. Remove all the seeds and the white pith from the peppers and cut them into diagonal pieces about 2.5cm/1 inch.

4. Heat the oil in a heavy frying pan over medium high heat. Add the celery and stir-fry until barely tender.

5. Add courgettes and peppers and stir-fry until all the vegetables are tender crisp.

6. Add the salt, pepper and oregano or marjoram and cook for 30 seconds more. Stir in chives and serve immediately.

Step 3 Seed the peppers and cut them into strips. Cut the strips into 2.5cm/1 inch diagonal pieces.

Step 6 Stir-fry all the vegetables, seasonings and herbs until the vegetables are tender crisp.

Cook's Notes

Time
Preparation takes about 25 minutes and cooking takes about 5 minutes.

Preparation
The cooking time for this dish is short, so have everything prepared before actual cooking begins.

Serving Ideas
Serve hot as an accompaniment to Fried Chicken, Cola Glazed Ham or with Stuffed Poussins. Vegetables may also be served cold as a salad with a dash of lemon or vinegar added.

SERVES 4

WILD RICE PILAFF

Wild rice adds a nutty taste and a texture contrast
to rice pilaff. It's good as a side dish or stuffing.

120g/4oz uncooked long-grain rice, rinsed
60g/2oz wild rice, rinsed
15ml/1 tbsp oil
15ml/1 tbsp butter or margarine
2 sticks celery, finely chopped
2 spring onions
60g/4 tbsps chopped walnuts or pecans
60g/4 tbsps raisins
430ml/¾ pint chicken or vegetable stock

1. Heat the oil in a frying pan and drop in the butter.

2. When foaming, add both types of rice.

3. Cook until the white rice looks clear.

4. Add celery and chop the spring onions, reserving the dark green tops to use as a garnish. Add the white part of the onions to the rice and celery and cook briefly to soften.

5. Add the walnuts or pecans, raisins and stock. Bring to the boil, cover and cook until the rice absorbs the liquid and is tender. Sprinkle with reserved chopped onion tops.

Step 3 Cook both rices in butter and oil until the white rice looks clear. Stir constantly.

Step 5 Add remaining ingredients and, if desired, transfer to an ovenproof casserole for the remainder of cooking.

Cook's Notes

Time
Preparation takes about 25 minutes and cooking takes about 20 minutes.

Preparation
This pilaff may also be cooked in the oven in the same manner as Spaghetti Rice.

Serving Ideas
Delicious served as a side dish for chicken or used as a stuffing for Cornish hens or other small game birds.

SERVES 4-6

MINTED MIXED VEGETABLES

Carrots, cucumber and courgettes are all
complemented by the taste of fresh mint.
In fact, most vegetables are, so experiment.

3 medium carrots
1 cucumber
2 courgettes
140ml/¼ pint water
5ml/1 tsp sugar
Pinch salt
25g/1½ tbsps butter, cut into small pieces
15ml/1 tbsp coarsely chopped fresh mint leaves

Step 5 Combine all the vegetables and cook until liquid is almost evaporated.

Step 2 Peel the cucumber, quarter it and remove the seed before cutting into sticks.

Step 5 Add the butter, cut in small pieces and stir while the liquid evaporates.

1. Peel the carrots and cut them into sticks about 1.25cm/½ inch thick and 6.25cm/2½ inches long.

2. Peel the cucumber and cut it into quarters. Remove the centres and cut into sticks the same size as the carrots.

3. Cut the courgettes into sticks the same size as the other vegetables.

4. Combine the carrots, water, sugar and salt in a medium saucepan. Cover the pan and bring to the boil over high heat. Reduce the heat to medium and cook for about 3 minutes. Uncover the pan and cook a further 3 minutes.

5. Increase the heat and add the cucumber and courgettes and boil until the vegetables are tender crisp. Add the butter and stir over heat until melted and the liquid has completely evaporated, glazing the vegetables. Remove from the heat, add the mint and toss well.

Cook's Notes

Time
Preparation takes about 25-30 minutes and cooking takes about 6-10 minutes.

Variation
Other root vegetables such as parsnips or swedes may be used instead of or in addition to the carrots.

Preparation
If the vegetables are cooking faster than the liquid is evaporating, pour off some of the liquid and continue to cook until completely evaporated.

SERVES 4-6

OKRA FRITTERS

This vegetable, often used in Indian cookery, is otherwise rather neglected. In this case, deep-frying complements okras' succulent texture.

225g/8oz yellow cornmeal
5ml/1 tsp salt
2 eggs, beaten
675g/1½lbs fresh okra, washed, stemmed and cut
   crossways into 1.25cm/½ inch thick slices
570ml/1 pint oil for frying

Step 4 Remove the okra from the oil with a draining spoon and place on paper towels.

Step 1 Dredge the egg-coated sliced okra in the cornmeal and salt mixture.

1. Combine the cornmeal and salt on a plate. Coat okra pieces in the beaten egg. Dredge the okra in the mixture.

2. Place the oil in a large, deep sauté pan and place over moderate heat.

3. When the temperature reaches 180°C/375°F add the okra in batches and fry until golden brown.

4. Drain thoroughly on paper towels and serve immediately.

Cook's Notes

 Time
Preparation takes about 15-20 minutes and cooking takes about 3 minutes per batch.

 Preparation
Do not coat the okra in the cornmeal too soon before cooking. If allowed to stand, cornmeal will become soggy.

Variation
Small okra can be coated and fried whole.

SERVES 4

HERBED VEGETABLE STRIPS

2 large courgettes, ends trimmed
2 medium carrots, peeled
1 large or 2 small leeks, trimmed, halved and well washed
120g/4oz walnuts
1 small onion, chopped
30g/2 tbsps chopped parsley
15g/1 tbsp dried basil
280-400ml/½-¾ pint olive oil
Salt and pepper

1. Cut the courgettes and carrots into long, thin slices with a mandolin or by hand. A food processor will work but the slices will be short.

2. Cut the leeks into lengths the same size as the courgettes and carrots. Make sure the leeks are well rinsed in between all layers. Cut into long, thin strips.

3. Using a large, sharp knife, cut the courgette and carrot slices into long, thin strips about the thickness of 2 matchsticks. The julienne blade of a food processor will produce strips that are too fine to use.

4. Place the carrot strips in a pan of boiling salted water and cook for about 3-4 minutes or until tender crisp. Drain and rinse under cold water. Cook the courgette strips

separately for about 2-3 minutes and add the leek strips during the last 1 minute of cooking. Drain and rinse the vegetables and leave with the carrots to drain dry.

5. Place the walnuts, onion, parsley and basil in the bowl of a food processor or in a blender and chop finely.

6. Reserve about 45ml/3 tbsps of the olive oil for later use. With the machine running, pour the remaining oil through the funnel in a thin, steady stream. Use enough oil to bring the mixture to the consistency of mayonnaise. Add seasoning to taste.

7. Place reserved oil in a large pan and, when hot, add the drained vegetables. Season and toss over moderate heat until heated through. Add the herb and walnut sauce and toss gently to coat the vegetables. Serve immediately.

Step 3 Stack several lengths of courgette and carrot and cut into long julienne strips.

Cook's Notes

 Time
Preparation takes about 30-40 minutes and cooking takes about 45 minutes.

 Serving Ideas
Serve as a side dish with grilled meat, poultry or fish and prepare larger quantities for a vegetarian main course. Parmesan cheese may be sprinkled on top.

 Preparation
The sauce can be prepared several days in advance and kept, covered, in the refrigerator. It can also be frozen for up to 6 months.

SERVES 6

HERB RICE PILAFF

Fresh herbs are a must for this rice dish, but use whatever
mixture suits your taste or complements the main course.

30ml/2 tbsps oil
30g/2 tbsps butter
180g/6oz uncooked long-grain rice
570ml/1 pint boiling water
Pinch salt and pepper
90g/3oz mixed chopped fresh herbs (parsley, thyme,
    marjoram, basil)
1 small bunch spring onions, finely chopped

Step 3 Cook very gently for about 20 minutes, or until all the liquid has been absorbed by the rice and the grains are tender.

Step 1 Cook the rice in the oil and butter until it begins to turn opaque.

Step 4 Stir the onions and herbs into the rice and fluff up the grains with a fork.

1. Heat the oil in a large, heavy-based saucepan and add
the butter. When foaming, add the rice and cook over
moderate heat for about 2 minutes, stirring constantly.

2. When the rice begins to look opaque, add the water, salt
and pepper and bring to the boil, stirring occasionally.

3. Cover the pan and reduce the heat. Simmer very gently,

without stirring, for about 20 minutes or until all the liquid
has been absorbed and the rice is tender.

4. Chop the herbs very finely and stir into the rice along
with the chopped spring onions. Cover the pan and leave to
stand for about 5 minutes before serving.

Cook's Notes

Time
Preparation takes about 20 minutes and cooking takes about 20-25 minutes.

Serving Ideas
Serve as a side dish to any meat, poultry or game recipe.

Cook's Tip
The rice must simmer very slowly if it is to absorb all the water without overcooking. Add extra water or pour some off as necessary during cooking, depending on how much liquid the rice has absorbed.

SERVES 6

STUFFED COURGETTES

Courgettes can be stuffed with many different combinations. This one happens to be quite light.

6 even-sized courgettes
120g/4oz cottage cheese, drained
120g/4oz grated red Leicester cheese
1 small red pepper, seeded and chopped
30ml/2 tbsps chopped parsley
Pinch salt and cayenne pepper
1 large egg
Watercress or parsley to garnish

3. Chop the flesh and mix with the remaining ingredients.

4. Spoon filling into the shells and arrange in a greased baking dish. Bake, uncovered, in a pre-heated 180°C/350°F/Gas Mark 4 oven for 15 minutes. Grill, if desired, to brown the top. Garnish with watercress or parsley.

Step 4 Use a small spoon to fill the courgettes neatly.

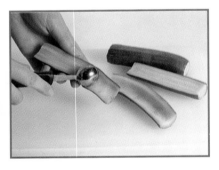

Step 2 Cut the pre-cooked courgettes in half lengthwise and scoop out the centre with a teaspoon or melon baller.

Step 4 Bake until the cheese melts and the filling begins to bubble slightly. Grill at this point, if desired.

1. Trim the ends of the courgettes and cook in boiling salted water for about 8 minutes, or steam for 10 minutes.

2. Remove from the water or steamer and cut in half. Allow to cool slightly and then scoop out the centre, leaving a narrow margin of flesh on the skin to form a shell. Invert each courgette slipper onto a paper towel to drain, reserving the scooped-out flesh.

Cook's Notes

Time
Preparation takes about 30 minutes and cooking takes about 23-25 minutes.

Preparation
The dish may be prepared ahead of time and kept in the refrigerator overnight to bake the next day.

Serving Ideas
Serve as a vegetable side dish with meat, poultry of fish. Alternatively, serve as a starter. Double the quantity and serve as a vegetarian main course.

Watchpoint
Be sure the courgettes are very well drained before filling. Baking will draw out any excess moisture and make the dish watery.

SERVES 6-8

BAKED BEANS

Treacle gives a different taste to
everyone's favourite snack.

450g/1lb dried haricot beans
1.5 litres/2½ pints water
120g/4oz belly pork
1 onion, peeled and left whole
5ml/1 tsp dry mustard
90ml/6 tbsps treacle
Salt and pepper

3. Bake in a pre-heated 160°C/300°F/Gas Mark 2 oven for about 2 hours. Add the remaining liquid, stirring well, and cook a further 1½ hours, or until the beans are tender. Uncover the beans for the last 30 minutes.

4. To serve, remove and discard the onion. Take out the belly pork and remove the rind. Slice or dice the meat and return to the beans. Check the seasoning and serve.

Step 1 Soak the beans overnight so that they soften slightly and swell in size.

1. Soak the beans overnight in the water. Transfer to fresh water to cover. Bring to the boil and allow to cook for about 10 minutes. Drain and reserve the liquid.

2. Place the beans, belly pork and whole onion in a large, deep casserole or bean pot. Mix the treacle, mustard, salt and pepper with 280ml/½ pint of the reserved bean liquid. Stir into the beans and add enough bean liquid to cover. Expose only the rind on the belly pork and cover the casserole.

Step 2 Combine the beans, belly pork and onion with the treacle mixture.

Step 3 After the beans have baked for 2 hours, add remaining bean cooking liquid and stir well.

Cook's Notes

 **Time**
Preparation takes about 20 minutes, with overnight soaking for the beans. Alternatively, bring the beans to the boil and then allow to stand for 2 hours. Cook as directed in the recipe. Total cooking takes about 3½ hours.

 Preparation
The beans may be prepared well in advance and reheated just before serving. Leftovers may be frozen for up to 3 months.

Serving Ideas
Sausages may be served with the beans, if desired.

238

SERVES 4

CREAMED ONIONS

Whole button onions in a creamy, rich sauce complement poultry, meat and fish perfectly.

450g/1lb button onions
Boiling water to cover
570ml/1 pint milk
1 bay leaf
1 blade mace
30g/2 tbsps butter or margarine
30g/2 tbsps flour
Pinch salt and white pepper
Chopped parsley (optional)

Step 2 Once the onions are boiled, put them into cold water and the peels should come off easily.

Step 1 Trim down the root ends of each onion.

Step 3 Place the blade of mace and bay leaf in a saucepan with the milk and heat until just beginning to boil.

1. Trim the root hairs on the onions but do not cut the roots off completely. Place the onions in a large saucepan and pour over the boiling water. Bring the onions back to the boil and cook for about 10 minutes.

2. Transfer the onions to cold water, allow to cool completely and then peel off the skins, removing roots as well. Leave the onions to drain dry.

3. Place the milk in a deep saucepan and add the blade mace and the bay leaf. Bring just to the boil, take off the heat and allow to stand for 15 minutes.

4. Melt the butter in a large saucepan and, when foaming, stir in the flour. Strain on the milk and discard the bay leaf and blade mace. Stir well and bring to the boil. Allow the sauce to simmer for about 3 minutes to thicken. Add salt and white pepper to taste and stir in the onions. Cook to heat through, but do not allow the sauce to boil again. Serve immediately and garnish with chopped parsley, if desired.

Cook's Notes

Time
Preparation takes about 30 minutes and cooking takes about 10 minutes for the onions and about 10 minutes for the sauce.

Preparation
Infusing the milk with the bay leaf and blade mace gives extra flavour to the sauce.

Cook's Tip
When adding onions to a white sauce, do not allow the sauce to boil as the onions can cause it to curdle.

SERVES 6

SWEET-SOUR BEETROOT

An unusual recipe using this readily
available root vegetable. The colour makes this
a perfect accompaniment to plain meat or poultry.

900g/2lbs small beetroot
Boiling water
45g/3 tbsps cornflour
120g/4oz sugar
Pinch salt and pepper
280ml/½ pint white wine vinegar
180ml/6 fl oz reserved beet cooking liquid
30g/2 tbsps butter

Step 3 Slice the beetroots into thin rounds.

Step 3 The peel should pull easily off the beetroots with a sharp knife.

Step 4 Combine all the sauce ingredients and cook until the cornflour thickens and clears.

1. Choose even-sized beetroot and cut off the tops, if necessary. Place beetroot in a large saucepan of water. Cover the pan and bring to the boil. Lower the heat and cook gently until tender, about 30-40 minutes. Add more boiling water as necessary during cooking.

2. Drain the beetroot, reserving the liquid, and allow the beetroot to cool.

3. When the beetroot is cool, peel it and slice into 5mm/¼ inch rounds, or cut into small dice.

4. Combine the cornflour, sugar, salt and pepper, vinegar and required amount of beetroot liquid in a large saucepan. Bring to the boil over moderate heat, stirring constantly until thickened. Return the beetroot to the saucepan and allow to heat through for about 5 minutes. Stir in the butter and serve immediately.

Cook's Notes

Time
Preparation takes about 20 minutes, and cooking takes about 30-40 minutes for the beets, 5 minutes for the sauce and 5 minutes to reheat.

Preparation
Canned beetroot may also be used. Substitute canned juice for cooking liquid. Omit the 30-40 minutes cooking time and simply reheat in sauce.

Variation
Orange juice may be substituted for part of the vinegar measurement, if desired. Garnish with fresh orange slices for colour.

SERVES 6

CREAMY SWEETCORN AND PEPPERS

Sweetcorn is essential to this recipe, but other vegetables can be added, too. Choose your favourites or use what you have to hand.

60ml/4 tbsps oil
30g/2 tbsps butter or margarine
2 medium-size onions, peeled and finely chopped
1 clove garlic, crushed
1 medium-size green pepper, seeded and cut into small dice
6 tomatoes, peeled, seeded and diced
225g/8oz fresh corn kernels or frozen corn
280ml/½ pint chicken or vegetable stock
Pinch salt
60ml/4 tbsps double cream
Pinch of paprika

Step 1 Cook the onions and garlic until soft and transparent but not browned.

1. Heat the oil in a large casserole and add the butter. When foaming, add the onions and garlic and cook, stirring frequently, for about 5 minutes or until both are soft and transparent but not browned.

2. Add the green pepper, tomatoes, corn and stock. Bring to the boil over high heat.

3. Reduce the heat, partially cover the casserole and allow to cook slowly for about 10 minutes, or until the corn is tender. Add salt and stir in the cream. Heat through, sprinkle with paprika and serve immediately.

Step 2 Add the vegetables and liquid to the onions and cook until the corn is tender.

Step 3 Stir in the cream and return to the heat to warm through. Serve immediately.

Cook's Notes

Time
Preparation takes about 25 minutes. Cooking takes about 10 minutes for frozen corn and slightly longer for fresh corn.

Variation
Use canned tomatoes, coarsely chopped. Make up the tomato liquid to the required measurement with water.

Cook's Tip
Sweetcorn toughens if cooked at too high a temperature for too long, or if boiled too rapidly.

SERVES 4

SPAGHETTI RICE

An unusual combination of pasta and rice
make a deliciously different side dish.

120g/4oz uncooked long grain rice
120g/4oz uncooked spaghetti, broken into 5cm/2"
   pieces
45ml/3 tbsps oil
60ml/4 tbsps sesame seeds
30ml/2 tbsps chopped chives
Salt and pepper
430ml/¾ pint chicken, beef or vegetable stock
15ml/1 tbsp soy sauce
30ml/2 tbsps chopped parsley

1. Rinse the rice and pasta to remove starch, and leave to drain dry.

2. Heat the oil in a large frying pan and add the dried rice and pasta. Cook over moderate heat to brown the rice and pasta, stirring continuously.

3. Add the sesame seeds and cook until the rice, pasta and seeds are golden brown.

4. Add the chives, salt and pepper, and pour over 280ml/½ pint stock. Stir in the soy sauce and bring to the boil.

5. Cover and cook about 20 minutes, or until the rice and pasta are tender and the stock is absorbed. Add more of the reserved stock as necessary. Do not let the rice and pasta dry out during cooking.

6. Fluff up the grains of rice with a fork and sprinkle with the parsley before serving.

Step 2 Cook the rice and pasta in the oil until just beginning to brown.

Step 3 Add the sesame seeds and cook until the rice, pasta and seeds are golden brown.

Step 5 Cook until all the liquid is absorbed and the pasta and rice are tender.

Cook's Notes

 Time
Preparation takes about 25 minutes and cooking takes about 20 minutes or more.

 Preparation
If desired, once the stock is added the mixture may be cooked in a pre-heated 190°C/375°F/Gas Mark 5 oven. Cook for about 20 minutes, checking the level of liquid occasionally and adding more stock if necessary.

Serving Ideas
Serve as a side dish with meat or poultry. Give it an Italian flavour by omitting sesame seeds, chives and soy sauce. Substitute Parmesan and basil instead.

SERVES 4

STUFFED AUBERGINES

These are a good suggestion for either starters
or light meals. Prawns are delicious in the
filling, but other ingredients substitute well.

2 aubergines
90g/6 tbsps butter or margarine
1 onion, finely chopped
1 stick celery, finely chopped
1 small red pepper, seeded and chopped
1 clove garlic, crushed
Salt and pepper
120g/4oz cooked, peeled prawns
Dry breadcrumbs

Step 2 Using a small knife or teaspoon, scoop out the centre of the aubergine, leaving a thin border to form a shell.

Step 1 Cut the aubergines in half lengthwise, score the surface lightly with a sharp knife and sprinkle with salt.

Step 3 Spoon the filling carefully into the aubergine shells, mounding it slightly on top.

1. Cut the aubergines in half lengthwise and remove the stems. Score the cut surface lightly and sprinkle with salt. Leave the aubergines to stand on paper towels for 30 minutes. Rinse, pat dry and wrap in foil. Bake for 15 minutes in a preheated 180°C/350°F/Gas Mark 4 oven.

2. Scoop out the centre of the baked aubergines, leaving a margin of 5mm/¼ inch flesh inside the skins to form a

shell. Chop the scooped out flesh roughly. Melt the butter and add the chopped aubergine, onion, celery, pepper and garlic. Cook slowly to soften the vegetables.

3. Season with salt and pepper and add the prawns. Spoon the mixture into the shells, sprinkle with breadcrumbs and bake in an ovenproof dish for an additional 20 minutes. Serve hot.

Cook's Notes

Time
Preparation takes 30 minutes and cooking takes about 35 minutes.

Cook's Tip
Sprinkling aubergines with salt and leaving them to stand draws out the bitter juices, making them easier to digest and better tasting.

Serving Ideas
Serve as a first course or as a vegetable side dish.

SERVES 4

BAKED TOMATOES

A perfect side dish for grilled chicken
or fish, this is especially good for summer,
when tomatoes are at their best.

4 large ripe tomatoes
1 small green pepper, seeded and thinly sliced
4 spring onions, sliced
1 clove garlic, crushed
60ml/4 tbsps white wine or water
Salt
15g/1 tbsp butter or margarine
60ml/4 tbsps double cream

Step 3 Remove the peel in strips, starting at the stem end.

Step 1 Place tomatoes in a pan of boiling water.

Step 4 Cut in half through the stem end. Scoop out seeds with a small spoon.

1. Remove the tomato stems and place tomatoes in a pan of boiling water.

2. Leave for 30 seconds and remove with a draining spoon. Place immediately in a bowl of ice cold water.

3. Use a small, sharp knife to remove the peel, beginning at the stem end.

4. Cut the tomatoes in half and scoop out the seeds. Strain the juice and reserve it, discarding the seeds.

5. Place tomatoes cut side down in a baking dish and sprinkle over the reserved juice. Add the sliced pepper, onions, garlic, wine or water and salt. Dot with butter or margarine.

6. Place in a preheated 180°C/350°F/Gas Mark 4 oven for about 15-20 minutes, or until tomatoes are heated through and tender, but not falling apart. Strain juices into a small saucepan.

7. Bring juices to the boil to reduce slightly. Stir in the cream and reboil. Spoon over the tomatoes to serve.

Cook's Notes

Time
Preparation takes about 30 minutes and cooking takes 15-20 minutes

Preparation
Once the cream is added to the tomato liquid, allow the mixture to come just to the boil. Boiling rapidly at this stage can cause curdling.

Cook's Tip
Placing tomatoes into boiling water for 30 seconds and then into cold loosens the peel. This process works well with peaches, too.

SERVES 4-6

CRUNCHY TOPPED CAULIFLOWER

A crunchy almond and golden fried breadcrumb topping
brightens up a plain boiled cauliflower.

1 large head cauliflower
60g/4 tbsps butter or margarine
60g/4 tbsps finely chopped blanched almonds
60g/4 tbsps dry breadcrumbs
2 hard-boiled eggs
Chopped parsley and fresh dill

1. Remove the large coarse green leaves from the outside of the cauliflower. If desired, leave the fine pale green leaves attached.

2. Trim the stem and wash the cauliflower well.

3. Place the whole cauliflower in boiling water right side up. Add salt and bay leaf to the water and bring back to the boil. Cook the cauliflower for 12-15 minutes, or until just tender.

4. Melt the butter in a small frying pan and add the almonds. Cook slowly to brown. Stir in the breadcrumbs and cook about 1 minute or until crisp.

Step 1 Cut away the coarse green leaves with a sharp knife.

Step 3 Place right side up in a pan of boiling water.

Step 4 Melt the butter in a small pan and add the almonds. Cook slowly to brown, stir in the breadcrumbs and cook for 1 minutes, or until crisp.

5. Peel the eggs and cut them in half. Remove the yolks and cut the whites into thin strips. Press the yolks through a strainer.

6. When the cauliflower is cooked, drain it and place on serving dish. Spoon the breadcrumbs and almond topping over the cauliflower. Arrange the sliced egg white around the base of the cauliflower and sprinkle the egg yolks over the breadcrumb topping. Sprinkle over chopped parsley and dill. Serve immediately.

Cook's Notes

Time
Preparation takes about 20 minutes, cooking takes about 12-15 minutes.

Cook's Tip
Adding a bay leaf to the water when cooking cauliflower helps to neutralise the strong smell.

Watchpoint
Do not overcook cauliflower. It becomes watery very quickly.

SERVES 6

CREAMY POTATO BAKE

So creamy and delicious, this potato
dish makes any meal special.

1 clove garlic, peeled and crushed with the flat of a knife
30g/1oz butter
1kg/2¼lbs potatoes, peeled and thinly sliced
140ml/¼ pint single cream
Salt and pepper
180g/6oz grated cheese
90g/3oz butter or margarine cut into very small dice

1. Preheat the oven to 200°C/400°F/Gas Mark 6. Rub the
bottom and sides of a heavy baking dish with the crushed
clove of garlic. Grease the bottom and sides liberally with
the butter or margarine. Use a dish that can also be
employed as a serving dish.

2. Spread half of the potato slices in the bottom of the dish,
sprinkle with cheese, salt and pepper and dot with the
butter or margarine dice. Top with the remaining slices of

Step 1 Rub the
dish with the
garlic and butter.

Step 2 Layer the
potatoes with
cheese and
seasonings.

Step 3 Pour
cream into the
side of the dish.

potato, neatly arranged. Sprinkle with the remaining
cheese, salt, pepper and butter.

3. Pour the cream into the side of the dish around the
potatoes.

4. Cook in the top part of the oven for 30-40 minutes, or
until the potatoes are tender and the top is nicely browned.
Serve immediately.

Cook's Notes

Serving Ideas
A delicious side dish with
poultry or roast meats,
especially gammon.

Time
Preparation takes 25 minutes,
cooking takes 30-40 minutes.

Cook's Tip
Rubbing the dish with garlic
gives just a hint of flavour.

SERVES 6-8

SPICY RICE AND BEAN PILAFF

A lively side dish or vegetarian main course,
this recipe readily takes to creative variations
and even makes a good cold salad.

60ml/4 tbsps oil
225g/8oz long grain rice
1 onion, finely chopped
1 green pepper, seeded and chopped
5ml/1 tsp each ground cumin and coriander
Dash tabasco sauce
Salt
1 litre/1¾ pints vegetable stock
450g/1lb canned red kidney beans, drained and rinsed
450g/1lb canned tomatoes, drained and coarsely
   chopped
Chopped parsley

3. Add the tabasco, salt, stock and beans and bring to the boil. Cover and cook about 45 minutes, or until the rice is tender and most of the liquid is absorbed.

4. Remove from the heat and add the tomatoes, stirring them in gently. Leave to stand, covered, for 5 minutes.

5. Fluff up the mixture with a fork and sprinkle with parsley to serve.

Step 3 Cook with the remaining ingredients until rice is tender and most of the liquid is absorbed.

Step 2 Cook the rice in the oil until just turning opaque.

Step 4 Carefully stir in the tomatoes before covering and leaving to stand.

1. Heat the oil in a casserole or a large, deep saucepan.

2. Add the rice and cook until just turning opaque. Add the onion, pepper and cumin and coriander. Cook gently for a further 2 minutes.

Cook's Notes

Time
Preparation takes about 25 minutes and cooking takes about 50 minutes.

Serving Ideas
Serve with bread and a salad for a light vegetarian meal.
Serve as a side dish with meat or poultry, or cheese and egg dishes.

Variation
The recipe may be made with 450g/1lb fresh tomatoes, peeled, seeded and coarsely chopped.

SERVES 6-8

RATATOUILLE

Make this when summer vegetables are at
their best in flavour and price!

2 aubergines, sliced and scored on both sides
4-6 courgettes, depending on size
45-90ml/3-6 tbsps olive oil
2 onions, peeled and thinly sliced
2 green peppers, seeded and cut into 2.5cm/1 inch pieces
10ml/2 tsps chopped fresh basil or 5ml/1 tsp dried basil
1 large clove garlic, crushed
900g/2lbs ripe tomatoes, peeled and quartered
Salt and pepper
140ml/¼ pint dry white wine or stock

1. Lightly salt the aubergine slices and place on paper towels to drain for about 30 minutes. Rinse and pat dry. Slice the courgettes thickly and set them aside.

2. Pour 45ml/3 tbsps of the olive oil into a large frying pan and when hot, lightly brown the onions, green peppers and courgette slices. Remove the vegetables to a casserole and add the aubergine slices to the frying pan or saucepan. Cook to brown both sides lightly and place in the casserole with the other vegetables. Add extra oil while frying the vegetables as needed.

3. Add the garlic and tomatoes to the oil and cook for 1 minute. Add the garlic and tomatoes to the rest of the vegetables along with any remaining olive oil in the frying pan. Add basil, salt, pepper and wine or stock and bring to the boil over moderate heat. Cover and reduce to simmering. If the vegetables need moisture during cooking, add a little more wine or stock.

Step 1 Score and salt the aubergines and leave to drain.

Step 2 Brown all the vegetables lightly.

Step 3 Combine all the ingredients and simmer gently.

4. When the vegetables are tender, remove them from the casserole to a serving dish and boil any remaining liquid in the pan rapidly to reduce to about 30ml/2 tbsps. Pour over the ratatouille to serve.

Cook's Notes

Time
Leave aubergines to stand 30 minutes while preparing remaining vegetables. Cook combined ingredients for approximately 35 minutes.

Cook's Tip
Vegetables in this stew are traditionally served quite soft. If crisper vegetables are desired, shorten the cooking time but make sure the aubergine is thoroughly cooked.

SERVES 4

SPICY ORIENTAL NOODLES

A most versatile vegetable dish, this
goes well with meat or stands alone
for a vegetarian main course.

225g/8oz Chinese noodles (medium thickness)
75ml/5 tbsps oil
4 carrots, peeled
225g/8oz broccoli
12 Chinese mushrooms, soaked 30 minutes
1 clove garlic, peeled
4 spring onions, diagonally sliced
5-10ml/1-2 tsps chilli sauce, mild or hot
60ml/4 tbsps soy sauce
60ml/4 tbsps rice wine or dry sherry
10ml/2 tsps cornflour

1. Cook noodles in boiling salted water for about 4-5 minutes. Drain well, rinse under hot water to remove starch and drain again. Toss with about 15ml/1 tbsp of the oil to prevent sticking.

2. Using a large, sharp knife, slice the carrots thinly on the diagonal.

3. Cut the florets off the stems of the broccoli and divide into even-sized but not too small sections. Slice the stalks thinly on the diagonal. If they seem tough, peel them before slicing.

4. Place the vegetables in boiling water for about 2 minutes to blanch. Drain and rinse under cold water to stop the cooking, and leave to drain dry.

5. Remove and discard the mushroom stems and slice the caps thinly. Set aside with the onions.

6. Heat a wok and add the remaining oil with the garlic clove. Leave the garlic in the pan while the oil heats and then remove it. Add the carrots and broccoli and stir-fry about 1 minute. Add mushrooms and onions and continue to stir-fry, tossing the vegetables in the pan continuously.

7. Combine chilli sauce, soy sauce, wine and cornflour, mixing well. Pour over the vegetables and cook until the sauce clears. Toss with the noodles and heat them through and serve immediately.

Step 7 Cook vegetables and sauce ingredients until cornflour thickens and clears.

Cook's Notes

Time
Preparation takes about 25 minutes and cooking takes about 7-8 minutes.

Serving Ideas
Use as a side dish with chicken, meat or fish, or serve as a starter. May also be served cold as a salad.

SERVES 6

BUTTERED MIXED VEGETABLES

A tasty and colourful dish you
can make in no time at all!

120g/4oz fresh or frozen sweetcorn
120g/4oz fresh or frozen broad beans
120g/4oz fresh or frozen French beans
45g/3 tbsps butter
Salt and pepper
Chopped parsley

1. If using frozen vegetables, bring water to the boil in a saucepan and, when boiling, add the vegetables. Cook for about 5-8 minutes, drain and leave to dry.

2. If using fresh vegetables, bring water to the boil in a saucepan and add the broad beans first. After about 2 minutes, add the French beans. Follow these with the corn about 3 minutes before the end of cooking time. Drain and leave to dry.

3. Melt the butter in a saucepan and add the vegetables. Heat slowly, tossing or stirring occasionally, until heated through. Add salt and pepper to taste and stir in the parsley. Serve immediately.

Step 2 Cook all the vegetables in boiling water, adding them one after the other.

Step 3 Melt the butter in a saucepan and toss the vegetables over heat.

Cook's Notes

Time
Preparation takes about 10 minutes if using frozen vegetables and 25 minutes if using fresh vegetables. Cooking takes about 5-8 minutes for frozen vegetables and about 8-10 minutes for fresh vegetables.

Preparation
If using fresh vegetables, use a small, sharp knife to cut the kernels from the ears of the corn. Stand the corn on one end and cut down the length of the ear to separate the kernels. If using fresh broad beans, snap open the pods and push out the beans inside. If desired the outer skin of the beans may be removed after cooking. Top and tail the fresh French beans and cut into 2 or 3 pieces.

Variation
The recipe can be made with just corn and broad beans or corn and French beans. Add red or green pepper, or chopped onion for flavour variation.

MAKES 570ml/1 pint

RED PEPPER PRESERVES

This sweet but hot and spicy condiment
adds a bright spot of colour and
flavour to a main course or starter.

5 red peppers, seeded
3 red or green chillies, seeded
450g/12oz sugar
180ml/6 fl oz red wine vinegar
280ml/½ pint liquid pectin

Step 3 Add the chopped peppers and bring the mixture to the boil.

1. Chop the peppers and chillies finely in a food processor.

2. Combine the sugar and vinegar in a deep, heavy-based pan and heat gently to dissolve the sugar.

3. Add the peppers and bring the mixture to the boil. Simmer for about 15 or 20 minutes until reduced.

4. Stir in the pectin.

5. Pour into sterilised jars and seal. Keep for up to one year in a cool, dark place.

Step 4 Stir in the pectin and remove from the heat.

Cook's Notes

Preparation
To sterilise the storage jars, place them in boiling water and boil for 15 minutes. Drain the jars upside down on paper towels and then fill them with the hot preserves to within about 1.25cm/½ inch of the top. Pour a layer of melted wax directly on top of the preserves to seal. When preserves have cooled and the wax has solidified, cover the jars with their lids. Waxed paper discs may also be used. If desired, the sealing process may be omitted and the preserves stored tightly covered in the refrigerator. Refrigerator-stored preserves will not keep as long.

Time
Preparation takes about 20 minutes and cooking takes about 20-25 minutes.

Serving Ideas
Serve as a condiment with meat, poultry, vegetable, egg or cheese dishes.

MAKES 1 litre/2 pints

MIXED PEPPER RELISH

Prepare this colourful relish in the summer,
when peppers are plentiful, but save some
to brighten up winter meals, too.

1.5kg/3lbs sweet peppers (even numbers of red, green, yellow and orange, or as available), seeded
2 medium onions, finely chopped
2.5ml/½ tsp oregano
2.5ml/½ tsp ground coriander
2 bay leaves
Salt to taste
450g/1lb granulated or preserving sugar
430ml/¾ pint white wine vinegar or white distilled vinegar

Step 4 Drain the peppers and add them to the vinegar and sugar with the remaining ingredients.

Step 4 Spoon or ladle into sterilised preserving jars.

Step 2 Place the diced peppers and onions in a large saucepan and pour over enough water to barely cover.

1. Cut the peppers into small dice and combine with the onions in a large saucepan.

2. Pour over boiling water to cover, and return to the boil. Cook rapidly for 10 minutes and drain well.

3. Meanwhile, combine the sugar and vinegar in a large saucepan. Bring slowly to the boil to dissolve the sugar, stirring occasionally.

4. When the peppers and onions have drained, add them and the remaining ingredients to the vinegar and sugar. Bring back to the boil and then simmer for 30 minutes. Remove the bay leaves and pour into sterilised jars and seal.

Cook's Notes

Time
Preparation takes about 30 minutes and cooking takes about 45 minutes.

Preparation
Sterilise the jars for storage in the same way as for Red Pepper Preserves. Omit the covering of wax, and seal the jars immediately. Store in a cool, dark place for up to one year, or cover tightly and keep in the refrigerator for a shorter time.

Serving Ideas
Serve as a condiment with cheese, egg and meat dishes. Relish is also good served with fish or shellfish.

SERVES 6-8

CRANBERRY ORANGE SAUCE

Cranberries, with their crisp taste
and bright hue, are perfect with
ham, chicken, pork and turkey.

340g/12oz whole cranberries, fresh or frozen
Juice and rind of 2 large oranges
225g/8oz sugar

Step 2 Grate the oranges on the coarse side of a grater or use a zester to remove the rind.

1. Pick over the cranberries and remove any that are shrivelled or discoloured.

2. Use the coarse side of the grater to grate the oranges. Take care not to remove too much of the white pith. Alternatively, remove the rind with a zester. Cut the oranges in half and squeeze them for juice.

3. Combine the sugar and orange rind in a deep saucepan and strain in the orange juice to remove the seeds. Bring to the boil and simmer for about 3 minutes, stirring continuously to dissolve the sugar.

4. When the sugar has dissolved, add the cranberries and cook until the skins pop, about 5 minutes. Remove from the heat and allow to cool slightly before serving. The sauce may also be served chilled.

Step 3 Combine the orange juice, rind and sugar in a deep saucepan, bring to the boil and cook until the sugar dissolves.

Step 4 Add the cranberries and cook until the skins pop.

Cook's Notes

Time
Preparation takes about 15 minutes, and cooking takes about 10 minutes.

Variations
Cranberry sauce may be prepared without the orange. Simply substitute water for the orange juice. Alternatively, cook with red wine. Add cinnamon, cloves or allspice, if desired.

Preparation
Cranberry sauce may be prepared up to 1 week ahead of time and kept in the refrigerator, well covered.

MAKES 700ml/1¼ PINTS

NUTTY HORSERADISH SAUCE

This creamy, piquant sauce can be made with any
variety of nuts you choose. The recipe makes
a lot, but a sauce this good won't go to waste.

280ml/½ pint sour cream or natural yogurt
60ml/4 tbsps prepared horeseradish
30ml/2 tbsps white wine vinegar
15ml/1 tbsp whole grain mustard
Pinch salt, white pepper and sugar
280ml/½ pint whipping cream
90ml/6 tbsps finely chopped nuts

1. Combine sour cream or yogurt and horseradish in a small bowl. Add the vinegar, mustard, sugar, salt and pepper, and stir into the sour cream. Do not over-stir. Chill in the refrigerator for at least 2 hours.

2. Whip the cream until soft peaks form.

3. Mix the chopped nuts into the sour cream sauce and stir in a spoonful of cream to lighten the mixture. Fold in the remaining cream and serve chilled.

Step 1 Combine sour cream, horseradish, vinegar, mustard, sugar and seasoning. Stir carefully to mix.

Step 3 Fold in nuts and cream using a large spoon or spatula.

Cook's Notes

Time
Preparation takes about 15 minutes, with 2 hours chilling time.

Cook's Tip
Cream that has been refrigerated for at least 2 hours is easier to whip.

Serving Ideas
The sauce is good with cold poached salmon, seafood, cold roast beef or hot baked potatoes.

8

CAKES
&
BISCUITS

pages 274-299

SERVES 6

FLOURLESS CHOCOLATE CAKE

This is part mousse, part soufflé, part cake and completely heavenly!
It's light but rich, and adored by chocolate lovers everywhere.

450g/1lb plain chocolate
30ml/2 tbsps strong coffee
30ml/2 tbsps brandy
6 eggs
90g/6 tbsps sugar
280ml/½ pint whipping cream
Icing sugar
Fresh whole strawberries

1. Melt the chocolate in the top of a double boiler. Stir in the coffee and brandy and leave to cool slightly.

2. Break up the eggs and then, using an electric mixer, gradually beat in the sugar until the mixture is thick and mousse-like. When the beaters are lifted the mixture should mound slightly.

3. Whip the cream until soft peaks form.

4. Beat the chocolate until smooth and shiny, and gradually add the egg mixture to it.

5. Fold in the cream and pour the cake mixture into a well greased 22cm/9" deep cake pan with a disk of greaseproof paper in the bottom. Bake in a pre-heated

Step 5 Pour the cake mixture into the prepared pan and then place it in a bain marie.

180°C/350°F/Gas Mark 5 oven in a bain marie. To make a bain marie, use a roasting pan and fill with warm water to come halfway up the side of the cake pan.

6. Bake about 1 hour and then turn off the oven, leaving the cake inside to stand for 15 minutes. Loosen the sides of the cake carefully from the pan and allow the cake to cool completely before turning it out.

7. Invert the cake onto a serving plate and carefully peel off the paper. Place strips of greaseproof paper on top of the cake, leaving even spaces in betweeen the strips. Sprinkle the top with icing sugar and carefully lift off the paper strips to form a striped or chequerboard decoration. Decorate with whole strawberries.

Cook's Notes

Cook's Tip
Cooking a delicate cake mixture in a bain marie helps protect it from the direct heat of the oven, maintains a more even temperature and gives the cake a better texture.

Watchpoint
Do not allow the water around the cake to boil at any time. If it starts to bubble, pour in some cold water to reduce the temperature.

Preparation
If desired, the cake may be prepared a day in advance and can be left well-covered overnight. This will produce a denser texture.

MAKES 1 CAKE

SYRUP CAKE

Rather like gingerbread, but with a spicy taste of cinnamon,
nutmeg and cloves instead, this cake can be served
with coffee or tea or warm with cream as a pudding.

225g/8oz vegetable shortening
250ml/8 fl oz treacle
3 eggs, beaten
340g/12oz plain flour
15g/1 tbsp baking powder
Pinch salt
5ml/1 tsp cinnamon
1.25ml/¼ tsp ground nutmeg
Pinch ground cloves
60g/4 tbsps chopped nuts
60g/4 tbsps raisins

3. Stir in the nuts and raisins and pour the mixture into a lightly greased 13.5 x 32.5cm/9 x 13" baking pan.

4. Bake for about 45 minutes in a pre-heated 190°C/375°F/Gas Mark 5 oven.

5. To test for doneness, insert a skewer into the centre of the cake. If it comes out clean, the cake is done. Allow to cool and cut into squares to serve.

Step 2 Sift in the dry ingredients and combine by hand.

Step 1 Cream the shortening until light and fluffy. Beat in the treacle with an electric mixer.

Step 5 Insert a skewer into the centre of the cake. If it comes out clean the cake is done.

1. Cream the shortening until light and fluffy. Add the treacle and beat with an electric mixer. Add the eggs one at a time, beating well in between each addition.

2. Sift the flour together with a pinch of salt and baking powder. Combine with the treacle mixture and add the spices.

Cook's Notes

 Times
Preparation takes about 20 minutes and cooking takes about 45 minutes.

 Variation
The cake may be prepared without the nuts and raisins, if desired. Add vanilla essence or lemon rind, if desired, for extra flavour.

 Cook's Tip
Lightly oil the inside of the measuring cup when measuring syrups like treacle or molasses. The syrup will not stick to the cup but will pour right out.

MAKES 12

RAINBOW SUGAR BUNS

Pretty pastel coloured sugar dressed up
fruit buns that are as easy to make as
they are delicious to eat.

15g/1 tbsp dried active yeast
90ml/3 fl oz lukewarm water
10ml/2 tsps sugar
450g/1lb plain flour
60g/4 tbsps additional sugar
Pinch salt
5ml/1 tsp ground ginger
Grated rind of 1 lemon
2 eggs
90ml/6 tbsps lukewarm milk
60g/4 tbsps butter or margarine, cut in small pieces
120g/4oz sultanas, currants and chopped glacé fruit

Icing

180g/6oz granulated sugar
Purple, yellow and green food colourings
225g/8oz icing sugar
Juice of 1 lemon
Hot water

1. Sprinkle the yeast on top of the lukewarm water and stir in the sugar. Set in a warm place to prove for 15 minutes, or until bubbly.

2. Sift the flour, sugar, salt and ginger into a large bowl and add the lemon rind. Make a well in the centre of the ingredients and pour in the yeast. Add the egg and milk.

3. Beat well, drawing the flour in from the outside edge, and gradually add the butter, a few pieces at a time.

4. Turn the dough out onto a well-floured surface and knead until smooth and elastic, about 10 minutes. Place the dough in a large, lightly-oiled bowl and cover with oiled clingfilm.

5. Leave to rise in a warm place for 1-1½ hours or until doubled in bulk.

6. Knock the dough back and knead in the fruit to distribute it evenly.

7. Oil a 12-space patty tin. Divide the dough in 12 and knead each piece into a smooth ball. Place a ball in each space in the tin and cover lightly. Leave in a warm place for 20-30 minutes to rise a second time. Bake at 190°C/ 375°F/ Gas Mark 6 for about 20-25 minutes, or until golden brown. Allow to cool slightly and loosen the buns. Cool completely before removing from the tin.

8. Place an equal portion of granulated sugar in each of three jars and add a drop of different food colouring to each. Shake the jars to colour the sugar.

9. Sift the icing sugar and mix with the lemon juice. Add enough hot water to make an icing that pours easily but still clings to the back of a spoon. Spoon some icing over each bun and sprinkle the cakes with the different coloured sugars before the icing sets.

Step 6 When the dough has risen the first time, knock back and knead in the fruit to distribute them evenly.

Cook's Notes

Time
Preparation takes about 40 minutes. This does not include rising times for the yeast dough. Cooking takes about 20-25 minutes.

Variation
Use dried fruit such as apricots, dates or prunes, finely chopped, instead of glacé fruit. Nuts or chocolate chips may also be used.

Preparation
The buns may be prepared the day before and kept in airtight containers. Ice and decorate with sugar on the day of serving.

MAKES ABOUT 24

LEMON AND RAISIN TEA CAKES

Cooked rice is the surprise ingredient in these cakes that
are crisp outside, yet soft and light inside.

120g/4oz long-grain rice, cooked
120g/4oz plain flour
5ml/1 tsp baking powder
Pinch salt
120g/4oz sugar
2 eggs, separated
90ml/6 tbsps milk
Grated rind of 1 lemon
60g/4 tbsps raisins

5. Lightly oil the base of a heavy frying pan and place over moderate heat. When the pan is hot, drop in about 15ml/1 tbsp of batter and if necessary, spread into a small circle with the back of the spoon.

6. Cook until brown on one side and bubbles form on the top surface. Turn over and cook the other side. Cook 4-6 at a time.

7. Repeat until all the batter is used, keeping the cakes warm. Serve plain or buttered.

Step 4 Beat the egg whites until stiff peaks form.

Step 4 Mix a spoonful of whites into the rice mixture to lighten it. Fold in the remaining whites using a large spoon.

1. Cook the rice, rinse, drain and leave to cool completely.

2. Sift the flour, baking powder and salt into a mixing bowl and stir in the sugar.

3. Beat the yolks with the milk and add gradually to the dry ingredients, stirring constantly, to make a thick batter. Stir in the rice.

4. Beat the egg whites until stiff but not dry and fold into the batter along with the lemon rind and raisins.

Step 5 Drop the mixture by spoonfuls into a hot frying pan. Cook until brown on both sides.

Cook's Notes

Time
Preparation takes about 40 minutes and cooking takes about 40-45 minutes.

Cook's Tip
To drain rice thoroughly, place in a colander and make several drainage holes with the handle of a wooden spoon.

Serving Ideas
Squeeze lemon juice over hot tea cakes, or spoon on jam. Cakes can also be served cold.

MAKES 12

PECAN PASTRIES

These sweet, nutty pastries are
deep-fried to make them light
and crisp.

120g/4oz plain flour
5ml/1 tsp baking powder
1.25ml/¼ tsp salt
60ml/4 tbsps cold water
Oil for frying
280ml/½ pint golden syrup mixed with 140ml/¼ pint
    treacle
90g/3oz finely chopped pecans

Step 1 Sift the dry ingredients into a bowl and make a well in the centre.

1. Sift the flour, baking powder and salt together in a large bowl. Make a well in the centre and pour in the cold water.

2. Using a wooden spoon, mix until a stiff dough forms, and then knead by hand until smooth.

3. Divide the dough into 12 portions, each about the size of walnut. Roll out each portion of dough on a floured surface until very thin.

4. Heat the oil in a deep fat fryer to 180°C/350°F. Drop each piece of pastry into the hot fat using two forks. Twist the pastry just as it hits the oil. Cook one at a time until light brown.

5. In a large saucepan, boil the syrup until it forms a soft ball when dropped into cold water.

6. Drain the pastries on paper towels after frying and dip carefully into the hot syrup. Sprinkle with pecans before the syrup sets and allow to cool before serving.

Step 3 On a floured surface, roll out each piece until very thin.

Cook's Notes

Time
Preparation takes about 30 minutes and cooking takes about 2 minutes per pastry.

Cook's Tip
The pastries must be served on the day they are made because they do not keep well.

282

MAKES ABOUT 36

BROWN SUGAR BISCUITS

This rather thick dough bakes to a crisp
golden brown, perfect as an accompaniment
to ice cream or fruit salad.

300g/10oz light brown sugar
45ml/3 tbsps golden syrup
60ml/4 tbsps water
1 egg
250g/9oz plain flour
15ml/1 tbsp ground ginger
15ml/1 tbsp bicarbonate of soda
Pinch salt
120g/4oz finely chopped nuts

Step 1 Combine the sugar, syrup water and egg with an electric mixer until light.

1. Mix the brown sugar, syrup, water and egg together in a large bowl. Beat with an electric mixer until light.

2. Sift flour with the ginger, baking soda and salt into the brown sugar mixture and add the nuts. Stir by hand until thoroughly mixed.

3. Lightly oil three baking sheets and drop the mixture by spoonfuls about 5cm/2 inches apart.

4. Bake in a pre-heated 190°C/375°F/Gas Mark 5 oven until lightly browned around the edges, about 10-12 minutes. Leave on the baking sheet for 1-2 minutes before removing with a palette knife to a wire rack to cool completely.

Step 3 Use a spoon to drop the batter about 5cm/2 inches apart onto a greased baking sheet.

Step 4 Bake until browned around the edges. Cool slightly and remove with a palette knife.

Cook's Notes

Time
Preparation takes about 20 minutes and cooking takes about 10-12 minutes per batch.

Variation
Add raisins to the dough. Any variety of nuts will be good.

Preparation
The dough will keep in the refrigerator for several days. Allow to stand at room temperature for at least 15 minutes before using.

MAKES 1 LOAF

SPICED CRANBERRY NUT TEA BREAD

Tea breads don't rely on yeast to make them rise
so they are quick and easy to prepare.

225g/8oz plain flour
5ml/1 tsp baking powder
225g/8oz sugar
5ml/1 tsp baking soda
Pinch salt
1.25ml/¼ tsp ground nutmeg
1.25ml/¼ tsp ground ginger
120ml/4 fl oz orange juice
30g/2 tbsps butter or margarine, melted
60ml/4 tbsps water
1 egg
120g/4oz fresh cranberries, roughly chopped
120g/4oz hazelnuts, roughly chopped

Step 1 Sift the dry ingredients into a bowl and make a well in the centre.

1. Sift the dry ingredients and spices into a large mixing bowl. Make a well in the centre of the dry ingredients and pour in the orange juice, melted butter or margarine, water and egg. Using a wooden spoon, beat the liquid mixture, gradually drawing in the flour from the outside edge.

2. Add the cranberries and nuts and stir to mix.

3. Lightly grease a loaf pan about 22 x 12.5cm/ 9 x 5'. Press a strip of greaseproof paper on the base and up the sides. Lightly grease the paper and flour the whole inside of the pan. Spoon or pour in the bread mixture and bake in a pre-heated 170°C/325°F/Gas Mark 3 oven for about 1 hour, or until a skewer inserted into the centre of the loaf comes out clean.

4. Remove from the pan, carefully peel off the paper and cool on a wire rack. Lightly dust with icing sugar, if desired, and cut into slices to serve.

Step 1 Pour the liquid ingredients into the well and, using a wooden spoon, stir to gradually incorporate the flour from the outside edge.

Step 2 Fold in the cranberries and the nuts.

Cook's Notes

Time
Preparation takes about 25 minutes and cooking takes about 1 hour.

Watchpoint
Be sure to bake the bread mixture as soon as possible after the baking powder has been added or the bread will not rise the way it should.

Serving Ideas
Serve warm with butter or cream cheese with tea or coffee. May also be served cold.

MAKES 24-30

HAZELNUT FLORENTINES

Hazelnuts make a good alternative to almonds
in these crisp, toffee-like biscuits. They're a treat
with coffee or ice cream.

450g/1lb shelled and peeled hazelnuts
225g/8oz sugar
90ml/6 tbsps honey
90ml/6 tbsps double cream
225g/8oz butter
180g/6oz white chocolate, melted
180g/6oz plain chocolate, melted

1. Place hazelnuts in a plastic bag and tie securely. Tap nuts or roll them with a rolling pin to crush roughly.

2. Place sugar, honey, cream and butter in a heavy-based saucepan and heat gently to dissolve sugar. Bring to the boil and cook rapidly for about 1½ minutes. Remove from heat and stir in the nuts.

3. Brush baking sheets well with oil and spoon or pour out mixture in even amounts. Make only about six Florentines at a time.

4. Bake about 10 minutes in a pre-heated 190°C/375°F/Gas Mark 5 oven. Allow to cool on the baking sheets and, when nearly set, loosen with a palette knife and transfer to a flat surface to cool completely.

5. When all Florentines have been baked and cooled, melt both chocolates separately. Spread white chocolate on half of the Florentines and dark chocolate on the other half, or marble the two if desired.

6. Place chocolate side uppermost to cool slightly and then make a wavy pattern with the tines of a fork, or swirl chocolate with a knife until it sets in the desired pattern.

Step 3 Pour or spoon Florentine mixture into even rounds.

Step 4 Loosen partially-set Florentines with a palette knife.

Step 6 Use a fork to make a decorative pattern in partially set chocolate.

Cook's Notes

Time
Preparation takes about 45-50 minutes and cooking takes about 10 minutes per batch.

Freezing
Store well wrapped for up to 1 month. Unwrap and defrost chocolate side up at room temperature. Store in a cool place.

Serving Ideas
Make in small sizes, about 2-2.5cm/1½-2 inches, for petit fours.

SERVES 6

STRAWBERRY SHORTCAKE

Summer wouldn't be the same without a
delicious strawberry dessert. The scone-like
cakes can be made in advance.

225g/8oz plain flour
15ml/1 tbsp baking powder
Pinch salt
45g/3 tbsps sugar
90g/6 tbsps cream cheese, softened
45g/3 tbsps butter or margarine
1 egg, beaten
90-120ml/3-4 fl oz milk
Melted butter
450g/1lb fresh or frozen strawberries
Icing sugar
Juice of half an orange
280ml/½ pint whipped cream

1. Sift the flour, baking powder, salt and sugar into a large bowl.

2. Using 2 knives or forks, cut in the cheese and butter or margarine. A fod processor can also be used

3. Blend in the egg and enough milk to make a firm dough.

4. Knead lightly on a floured surface and then roll out to a thickness of 1.25cm/½ inch.

5. Cut the dough into an even number of 75cm/3 inch circles. Re-roll the trimmings and cut as before. Brush half of the circles with the melted butter and place the other halves on top, pressing down lightly. Bake on an ungreased baking sheet for about 15 minutes in a pre-heated 225°C/425°F Gas Mark 7 oven. Allow to cool slightly and then transfer to a wire rack.

6. Hull the strawberries and wash well. Purée half of them in a food processor with the orange juice. Add icing sugar to taste if desired. Cut the remaining strawberries in half and combine with the purée.

7. Separate the shortcakes in half and place the bottoms on serving plates. Spoon over the strawberries and sauce and pipe or spoon on the cream.

8. Sprinkle the tops of the shortcake with icing sugar and place on top of the cream. Serve slightly warm or at room temperature.

Step 5 Brush one half of the dough circles with butter and place the other halves on top, pressing down lightly.

Step 7 The shortcakes should separate in half easily with the help of a fork.

Cook's Notes

 Time
Preparation takes about 30-35 minutes and cooking takes about 15 minutes.

 Variation
Other fruit may be used to fill the shortcakes. Substitute peaches, apricots or other berries.

MAKES 24

NUT TARTLETS

Use what ever nuts you like best – walnuts,
pecans, even unsalted peanuts for
these very moreish treats.

Pastry
120g/4oz butter or margarine
90g/6 tbsps cream cheese
120g/4oz plain flour

Filling
90g/3oz chopped nuts
1 egg
180g/6oz light brown sugar
15g/1 tbsp softened butter
5ml/1 tsp vanilla essence
Icing sugar

1. Beat the butter or margarine and cheese together to soften.

2. Stir in the flour, adding more if necessary to make the dough easy to handle, although it will still be soft. If possible, roll the dough into 2.5cm/1 inch balls. Chill thoroughly on a plate.

3. Mix all the filling ingredients together thorougly, omitting icing sugar.

4. Place a ball of chilled dough into a small tart pan and, with floured fingers, press up the sides and over the base of the pans. Repeat with all the balls of dough.

5. Spoon in the filling and bake for about 20-25 minutes at 180°C/350°F Gas Mark 4.

6. Allow to cool about 5 minutes and remove carefully from the pans. Cool completely on a wire rack before sprinkling with icing sugar.

Step 2 Roll the dough into 2.5cm/1 inch balls and chill until firm.

Step 4 Place a ball of dough in a small tart pan and with floured fingers press up the sides and over the base.

Step 5 Use a teaspoon to fill the tart pans taking care not to get filling over the edge of the pastry.

Cook's Notes

Time
Preparation takes about 25 minutes. The dough will take at least 1 hour to chill thoroughly. Cooking takes about 20-25 minutes.

Preparation
If the dough is too soft to handle after mixing, chill for about 30 minutes or until easier to handle.

Serving Ideas
Serve with coffee or tea. The Tartlets can be made in a larger size and served as a pudding with whipped cream.

MAKES 12

CORN MEAL MUFFINS

A cross between cake and bread, these muffins are
slightly sweet and crumbly. They are nice with butter
or jam as a tea time treat or serve as you would hot rolls.

120g/4oz plain flour
60g/4 tbsps sugar
10ml/2 tsps baking powder
2.5ml/½ tsp salt
150g/5oz yellow cornmeal
1 egg, slightly beaten
60ml/4 tbsps oil
370ml/11 fl oz milk

Step 4 Beat the
liquid ingredients
in the well with a
wooden spoon,
gradually
incorporating the
dry ingredients.

Step 2 Sift the dry
ingredients into a
large bowl,
leaving a well in
the centre.

Step 5 Spoon the
batter into the
prepared pans. It
may be slightly
lumpy.

1. Pre-heat the oven to 250°C/450°F Gas Mark 8. Grease
a 12-space patty tin liberally with oil. Heat the pans for 5
minutes in the oven.

2. Sift the flour, sugar, baking powder and salt into a large
bowl. Add the cornmeal and stir to blend, leaving a well in
the centre.

3. Combine the egg, oil and milk and pour into the well.

4. Beat with a wooden spoon, gradually incorporating the
dry ingredients into the liquid. Do not overbeat the mixture.
It can be slightly lumpy.

5. Spoon the batter into the pans and bake for about 14
minutes.

6. Cool briefly in the pans and then remove to a wire rack
to cool further. Serve warm.

Cook's Notes

Time
Preparation takes about 20
minutes and cooking takes
about 14 minutes.

Variation
If you have a cast iron frying
pan, coat liberally with oil and
place in the oven to pre-heat. Pour the
batter into the pan and then bake. Cut
into wedges and serve directly from the
pan.

Freezing
Cornmeal muffins may be
baked and frozen well
wrapped for up to 2 months. Defrost at
room temperature and reheat wrapped
in foil for about 5 minutes in a moderate
oven. Do not overheat as the muffins
can dry out easily. Store well wrapped.

STEAMED BROWN BREAD

A very different kind of tea bread,
cooked in a tin can!

225g/8oz fine cornmeal
225g/8oz wholewheat flour
120g/4oz plain flour
Pinch salt
90ml/6 tbsps treacle mixed with 5ml/1 tsp bicarbonate of
  soda
430ml/¾ pint cold water
Butter or oil
Boiling water

Step 3 Fill the cans with the bread mixture to about two thirds full.

Step 3 Grease rinsed out cans generously with butter or margarine.

Step 4 Cover the tops of the cans tightly with foil and place on a rack in boiling water to come halfway up the sides.

1. Sift the dry ingredients into a large bowl and return the bran to the bowl.

2. Mix the treacle, bicarbonate of soda and water together. Make a well in the centre of the flour and pour in the mixture. Mix just until well blended.

3. Use a large can from canned tomatoes, coffee or canned fruit. Alternatively, use about 6 smaller cans. Wash them well and remove the labels. Grease generously with oil or butter. Spoon the bread mixture to

come about two thirds of the way up the sides of the cans.

4. Cover the tops of the cans tightly with buttered or oiled foil. Place them on a rack in a deep saucepan. Pour enough boiling water around the cans to come about halfway up the sides. Allow water to bubble gently to steam the bread for 3-4 hours in the covered pan. Add more boiling water as necessary during cooking.

5. The bread is ready when a skewer inserted into the centre of the bread comes out clean.

Cook's Notes

Time
Preparation takes about 20 minutes and cooking takes about 3-4 hours. Cooking time may be slightly shorter for smaller cans.

Variation
Raisins, chopped dates or prunes may be added to the bread mixture if desired.

Serving Ideas
Serve warm with butter or cream cheese.

MAKES 1 LOAF

CHOCOLATE CINNAMON SWEET BREAD

Pull this bread apart to serve in individual pieces rather than slicing it.
Savoury versions substitute Parmesan and herbs for sugar and spice.

Dough

60ml/4 tbsps warm water
15ml/1 tbsp sugar
1 envelope dry yeast
340-400g/12-14oz strong flour
90g/6 tbsps sugar
Pinch salt
75g/5 tbsps butter, softened
5 eggs

Topping

120g/4oz butter, melted
225g/8oz sugar
10ml/2 tsps cinnamon
10ml/2 tsps cocoa
90g/6 tbsps finely chopped nuts

1. Sprinkle 15ml/1 tbsp sugar and the yeast on top of the water and leave it in a warm place until foaming.

2. Sift 340g/12oz of flour into a bowl and add the sugar and salt. Rub in the butter until completely blended.

3. Add 2 eggs and the yeast mixture, mixing in well. Add the remaining eggs one at a time until the mixture forms a soft, spongy dough. Add remaining flour as necessary. Knead for 10 minutes on a lightly floured surface until smooth and elastic.

4. Place the dough in a greased bowl and turn over to grease all the surfaces. Cover loosely and put in a warm place. Leave to stand for 1-1½ hours or until doubled in bulk.

5. Butter a ring mould liberally. Knock the dough down and knead it again for about 5 minutes. Shape into balls about 5cm/2 inches in diameter. Mix the topping ingredients together except for the melted butter. Roll the dough balls in the butter and then in the sugar mixture.

6. Place a layer of dough balls in the bottom of the mould and continue until all the dough and topping has been used. Cover and allow to rise again about 15 minutes. Bake in a pre-heated 180°C/350°F/Gas Mark 4 oven for about 45-50 minutes. Loosen from the pan and turn out while still warm.

Step 5 Roll the dough in melted butter and then in the sugar mixture.

Step 6 Lay out the balls of dough in a prepared pan.

Cook's Notes

Time
Preparation takes about 2 hours and cooking takes about 45-50 minutes.

Cook's Tip
Check the temperature of the water carefully. If it is too hot it can kill the yeast and then the bread will not rise. Water should feel warm when tested on the inside of your wrist.

Serving Ideas
Serve warm with coffee or tea, or serve as an accompaniment to a fresh fruit salad.

9

DESSERTS

pages 302-351

SERVES 4

STRIPED SORBET

A tricoloured iced treat that can
be prepared well ahead, this is a
wonderful way to end a summer meal.

570ml/1 pint water
225g/8oz sugar
Juice of 1-2 lemons
8 kiwi fruit, peeled and roughly chopped
4 ripe bananas, peeled and roughly chopped
450g/1lb raspberries, fresh or well drained frozen
2 egg whites
1 banana, 1 kiwi fruit, sliced and whole raspberries to
  garnish

Step 8 Pour the banana sorbet on top of the frozen raspberry sorbet.

1. Combine the water and sugar in a heavy-based saucepan. Bring slowly to the boil to dissolve the sugar.

2. When the sugar is completely dissolved, boil the syrup rapidly for about 1 minute. Allow it to cool completely and then refrigerate until completely cold.

3. Purée the kiwi fruit in a food processor, sieving to remove the seeds if desired. Purée the bananas and the raspberries separately. Sieve the raspberries to remove the seeds.

4. Divide the cold syrup in 3 parts and mix each with one of the fruit purées. Taste each and add about 15-30ml/1-2 tbsps of lemon juice to each fruit syrup, depending on the sweetness of the fruit.

5. Freeze the fruit syrups separately until almost solid, about 2 hours, then mix again in the food processor to break up ice crystals. Freeze again separately until solid.

6. Whip the egg whites until stiff. Process the sorbets again, separately, dividing the egg white among all three.

7. Pour the raspberry sorbet into a bowl or mould and freeze until firm.

8. Pour the banana sorbet on top and freeze again.

9. Finish with the kiwi sorbet and freeze overnight or until firm.

10. To unmould, dip briefly in hot water and invert on a plate. Garnish with the prepared fruit.

Cook's Notes

Time
Preparation takes about 35 minutes. The sorbets will take at least 2 hours to freeze before their first mixing. Once layered, the sorbets should be allowed to freeze overnight.

Variation
Any kind of berries may be substituted for the raspberries or the kiwi fruit in the recipe. One small melon will also take the place of the kiwi fruit, if desired.

Preparation
The sorbets may also be prepared and frozen in an ice cream machine following the manufacturer's directions.

MAKES 1 CAKE

APPLE, PEAR OR PLUM CAKE

Cakes don't always have to be iced sponge
layers. This is made like a flan, using
a very versatile biscuit-like pastry.

Pastry

180g/6oz self-raising flour
Salt
45g/3 tbsp sugar
Dash vanilla essence or 5ml/1 tsp grated lemon rind
150g/5oz butter or margarine
2 egg yolks or 1 whole egg
15-30ml/1-2 tbsps milk or water

Filling

450g/1lb dessert apples, pears or plums
Sugar for dredging

Step 1 Rub the butter into the dry ingredients by hand or with a food processor until the mixture resembles fine breadcrumbs.

1. Sift the flour with the salt and sugar into a large bowl. Add the baking powder, if using, with the flour. Rub in the butter or margarine until the mixture resembles fine breadcrumbs.

2. Make a well in the centre and place in the egg yolks or the whole egg. Add the vanilla or lemon rind and 15ml/1 tbsp milk or water. Mix into the flour with a fork. If the pastry appears too dry, add the additional milk or water.

3. Knead together quickly with the hand to smooth out. If the mixture is too soft, wrap well and chill briefly.

4. Press the pastry on the base and up the sides of a flan dish, preferably one with a removable base. Chill 15 minutes.

5. Meanwhile, prepare the fruit. Peel, core and quarter the apples and slice thinly. Peel, core and quarter the pears and slice those thinly, lengthways. Cut the plums in half and remove the stones. Slice thinly. Arrange the chosen fruit on the base of the flan in straight lines or circles with the slices slightly overlapping. Sprinkle on sugar and bake in a preheated oven at 200°C/400°F/Gas Mark 6 until the pastry is pale golden brown and the fruit is soft. Allow to cool and sprinkle with additional sugar before serving.

Step 2 Make a well in the centre of the flour and place in the egg and milk or water. Mix together with a fork.

Step 3 Press the pastry into the flan dish, making sure the base and sides are of even thickness. Trim off any excess pastry around the edges.

Cook's Notes

Time
Preparation takes about 30 minutes, cooking takes about 35-40 minutes.

Cook's Tip
If the pastry begins to brown around the edges before the remaining pastry and fruit is cooked, cover the browned parts with foil, shiny side out.

Serving Ideas
Serve with whipped cream, ice cream or pouring cream. Custard sauce is also a nice accompaniment.

SERVES 6-8

STRAWBERRY TRIFLE

Summer means strawberries and this trifle
shows them off to good advantage.

30g/2 tbsps cornflour
570ml/1 pint milk
2 eggs, lightly beaten
30g/2 tbsps sugar
Grated rind of ½ a lemon
Pinch nutmeg
1 punnet ripe strawberries
16 sponge fingers
Sherry or brandy
140ml/¼ pint double cream

1. Mix the cornflour with some of the milk. Beat the eggs, sugar, lemon rind and nutmeg together and pour in the remaining milk. Mix with the cornflour mixture in a heavy-based pan and stir over gentle heat until the mixture thickens and comes to the boil.

2. Allow to boil for 1 minute or until the mixture coats the back of a spoon. Place a sheet of greaseproof paper directly on top of the custard and allow it to cool slightly.

3. Save 8 even-sized strawberries for garnish and hull the remaining ones. Place half of the sponge fingers in the bottom of a glass bowl and sprinkle with some of the sherry or brandy. Cut the strawberries in half and place a layer on top of the sponge fingers. Pour a layer of custard on top and repeat with the remaining sliced strawberries and sponge fingers. Top with another layer of custard and allow to cool completely.

4. Whip the cream and spread a thin layer over the top of the set custard. Pipe the remaining cream around the edge of the dish and decorate with the reserved strawberries. Serve chilled.

Step 1 Combine the custard ingredients in a heavy-based saucepan and cook until the mixture thickens and coats the back of a spoon.

Step 3 Place a layer of sponge fingers and strawberries in a serving dish and coat with a layer of custard. Repeat with remaining ingredients.

Step 4 Decorate the top using a piping bag fitted with a rosette nozzle.

Cook's Notes

Time
Preparation takes about 20 minutes, custard takes about 5 minutes to cook.

Variations
Decorate the top of the dessert with grated chocolate, toasted almonds or shelled pistachios in addition to, or instead of, the strawberries. Other fruit may be used, if desired.

STEAMED CRANBERRY PUDDING

Cranberries add a tangy taste to
a rich, satisfying pudding.

180g/6oz plain flour
10ml/2 tsps baking powder
Pinch salt
120g/4oz chopped cranberries
1 small piece stem ginger, finely chopped
2 eggs, well beaten
140ml/¼ pint honey
90ml/6 tbsps milk
Orange sauce
Grated juice and rind of 1 orange
Grated juice and rind of ½ lemon
120g/4oz sugar
15g/1 tbsp cornflour
180ml/6 fl oz water
15g/1 tbsp butter or margarine

1. Sift the dry ingredients together in a large bowl.

2. Toss in the cranberries and ginger.

3. Mix the eggs, honey and milk together and gradually stir into the dry ingredients and the cranberries. Do not over stir. The mixture should not be uniformly pink.

4. The mixture should be of thick dropping consistency. Add more milk if necessary.

5. Spoon the mixture into a well-buttered pudding basin or bowl, cover with buttered foil and tie the top securely.

6. Place the bowl on a rack in a pan of boiling water to come halfway up the sides. Cover the pan and steam the pudding for about 1½ hours, or until a skewer inserted into the centre comes out clean. Leave to cool in the basin or bowl for about 10 minutes, loosen the edge with a knife and turn out onto a plate.

7. Meanwhile, place the sugar and cornflour into a saucepan with the orange juice and rind and lemon juice and rind. Add the water, stirring to blend well. Bring to the boil and allow to simmer until clear. Beat in the butter at the end and serve with the pudding.

Step 3 Stir the liquid ingredients into the dry until well blended and of thick dropping consistency.

Step 5 Spoon into the prepared bowl or basin. Cover the top with foil and tie securely with string.

Cook's Notes

 Time
Preparation takes about 30-40 minutes and cooking takes about 1½ hours.

 Variation
If desired, use ground ginger instead of the stem ginger.

SERVES 4

CARAMEL ORANGES

This is one of the classic Italian restaurant sweets.
Vary the darkness of the caramel to suit
your taste, but watch it carefully!

4 large oranges
300g/10oz sugar
340ml/12 fl oz water
60ml/2 fl oz extra water

1. Use a swivel vegetable peeler to peel thin strips from two of the oranges. Take off any white pith and cut the strips into very thin julienne strips with a sharp knife.

2. Place the julienne strips in a small saucepan, cover with water and bring to the boil.

3. Peel all the oranges with a serrated-edged knife. Cut the ends off first and then take the peel and pith off in very thin strips using a sawing motion. Cut the oranges horizontally into slices about 5mm/¼ inch thick. Drain the orange peel strips and leave to dry. Combine sugar and water in a heavy-based pan. Reserve 60ml/2 fl oz water for later use. Place the mixture over medium heat until the sugar has dissolved. Add the drained orange peel strips to the pan.

4. Boil the syrup gently, uncovered, for about 10 minutes or until the orange strips are glazed. Remove the strips from the pan and place on a lightly oiled plate.

5. Return the pan to high heat and allow the syrup to boil, uncovered, until it turns a pale golden brown. Remove from the heat immediately and quickly add the extra water. Return to gentle heat and cook for a few minutes to dissolve hardened sugar. Remove the pan from the heat and allow to cool completely.

6. Arrange the orange slices in a serving dish and pour over the cooled syrup. Pile the glazed orange strips on top and refrigerate before serving.

Step 1 Peel the oranges into thin strips with a vegetable peeler. Remove any white pith and cut into thin julienne strips.

Step 3 Use a serrated knife to take off orange peel in thin strips.

Step 5 Cook the sugar and water to a pale golden brown syrup.

Cook's Notes

Time
Preparation takes about 25 minutes, cooking takes about 10 minutes to parboil the orange strips and about 10-15 minutes to caramelize the syrup.

Watchpoint
Keep a close eye on the syrup as it is caramelizing. It can burn very quickly.

Cook's Tip
All the white pith must be removed from the oranges and the orange strips or the whole dish will taste bitter.

SERVES 8

BREAD PUDDING WITH BRANDY SAUCE

A childhood pudding made sophisticated by the addition of a brandy-laced sauce, and a stylish presentation.

½ loaf day-old French bread
570ml/1 pint milk
3 eggs
90g/3oz raisins
5ml/1 tsp vanilla essence
Pinch ground ginger
Butter or margarine
120g/4oz butter
225g/8oz sugar
1 egg
60ml/4 tbsps brandy
Nutmeg

Step 2 Soak bread until very soft and mix with other ingredients.

1. Cut bread into small pieces and soak in the milk.

2. When the bread has softened, add the eggs, raisins, vanilla and ginger.

3. Grease 8 ramekin dishes with butter or margarine and fill each with an equal amount of pudding mixture to within 1.25cm/½ inch of the top.

4. Place the dishes in a roasting pan and pour in enough hot water to come halfway up the sides of the dishes. Bake in a preheated 180°C/350°F/Gas Mark 4 oven until risen and set – about 35-40 minutes.

5. When the puddings have cooked, combine the 120g/4oz butter and the sugar in the top of a double boiler and heat to dissolve the sugar.

6. Beat the egg and stir in a spoonful of the hot butter mixture. Add the egg to the double boiler and whisk over heat until thick. Allow to cool and add brandy.

7. To serve, turn out puddings onto plates and surround with sauce. Sprinkle the tops with nutmeg.

Step 4 Bake the pudding until risen and set. The puddings are done when a skewer inserted in the middle comes out clean.

Step 7 Loosen puddings from the sides of the dishes and turn out carefully.

Cook's Notes

Time
Preparation takes about 40 minutes, giving bread time to absorb milk. Cooking takes about 35-40 minutes for the pudding and about 20 minutes for the sauce.

Preparation
If desired, cook pudding in one large dish, increasing time to 1 hour. Spoon portions onto plates and pour over sauce.

Variation
Sauce may be prepared with lemon juice instead of brandy.

SERVES 4-6

CHERRY COMPÔTE

This makes a special, elegant pudding, but an easy one, too.
The contrast of hot brandied cherries and cold ice cream or
whipped cream is sensational.

675g/1½lbs black cherries, fresh or canned
30-60g/2-4 tbsps sugar
60ml/4 tbsp brandy
Vanilla ice cream or whipped cream

Step 1 Pit cherries using a cherry pitter, vegetable peeler or small knife.

1. If using fresh cherries, wash them, remove the stems and pit, if desired, but leave the cherries whole. Combine them with 60g/4 tbsps sugar in a saucepan and cook over gentle heat until the cherries soften and the juices run. If using canned cherries, combine the juice with 30g/2 tbsps sugar and heat through to dissolve the sugar. Pit the cherries, if desired, but leave them whole and add to the juice.

2. Pour the brandy into a separate saucepan or a large ladle. Heat the brandy and ignite with a match. Combine the brandy with the fruit and leave until the flames die down naturally.

3. Spoon the fruit over ice cream or on its own into serving dishes to be topped with whipped cream. Serve immediately.

Step 1 Cook slowly with the sugar until the cherries soften and juices run.

Step 2 Add brandy and cook briefly.

Cook's Notes

Time
Preparation takes about 30 minutes if pitting the cherries, and cooking takes about 10 minutes.

Preparation
If using fresh cherries, pit and cook in advance and set aside. Before adding the brandy, reheat the cherries until hot.

Buying Guide
£ Black cherries are often available already pitted in cans or bottles from larger supermarkets or speciality shops.

SERVES 6

APRICOT CHOUX PUFFS

These light puffs of choux pastry
are fried instead of baked.

90ml/6 tbsps water
15g/1 tbsp butter or margarine
90g/6 tbsps plain flour
3-4 eggs
Few drops vanilla essence
Icing sugar

Apricot Sauce

400g/14 canned apricots
15g/1 tbsp cornflour mixed with 60ml/4 tbsps water
Dash lemon juice

1. Combine the water and butter or margarine in a saucepan and slowly bring to the boil.

2. When boiling rapidly, stir in the flour quickly and remove the pan from the heat.

3. Beat in the eggs one at a time, beating well in between each addition. It may not be necessary to add all the eggs. The mixture should be of dropping consistency and hold its shape well. Beat in the vanilla essence.

4. Heat oil to 180°C/350°F in a deep fat fryer or in a deep saucepan on top of the stove. Drop the batter from a teaspoon into the hot fat and cook until puffed and golden. The choux puffs will rise to the surface of the oil when cooked and may be turned over if necessary. Cook the puffs about four at a time.

5. Drain on paper towels and dust with icing sugar.

6. While the choux puffs are cooking, combine all the sauce ingredients in a heavy-based pan and bring to the boil. Cook until thickened and then transfer to a blender or food processor and purie until smooth. Serve the sauce warm with the warm choux puffs.

Step 2 Add the flour to the boiling water and butter mixture, and stir until it leaves the sides of the pan.

Step 3 Beat in the eggs one at a time until the mixture is smooth and shiny and holds its shape.

Step 4 Drop the batter by spoonfuls into hot fat and cook until the puffs are brown and rise to the surface.

Cook's Notes

 Time
Preparation takes about 20 minutes. Choux puffs will take about 2 minutes to cook per batch.

Preparation
The choux puffs are best served as soon as they are cooked. They do not reheat well.

 Serving Ideas
Choux puffs may be served without the sauce with coffee or tea. Dust with icing sugar.

SERVES 4

BROWN SUGAR BANANAS

Bananas in a rich brown sugar sauce
make a delectable dessert.

4 ripe bananas, peeled
120g/4oz butter
120g/4oz soft brown sugar, light or dark
Pinch ground cinnamon and nutmeg
140ml/¼ pint orange juice
60ml/4 tbsps white or dark rum
Juice of ½ lemon
Whipped cream
Chopped pecans

Step 2 Combine butter, sugar and spices in a large frying pan and heat gently to form a syrup.

Step 1 Cut the bananas carefully in half lengthwise.

Step 3 Baste the bananas frequently whilst cooking, but do not turn them.

1. Cut the bananas in half lengthwise and sprinkle with lemon juice on all sides.

2. Melt the butter in a large frying pan and add the sugar, cinnamon, nutmeg and orange juice. Stir over gentle heat until the sugar dissolves into a syrup.

3. Add the banana halves and cook gently for about 3 minutes, basting the bananas often with syrup, but not turning them.

4. Once the bananas are heated through, warm the rum in a small saucepan or ladle and ignite with a match. Pour the flaming rum over the bananas and shake the pan gently until the flames die down naturally. Place 2 banana halves on a serving plate and top with some of the whipped cream. Sprinkle with pecans and serve immediately.

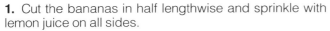

Cook's Notes

Time
Preparation takes about 15 minutes and cooking takes about 5 minutes for the sugar and butter syrup and 3-4 minutes for the bananas.

 Serving Ideas
The bananas may be served with vanilla ice cream instead of whipped cream, if desired.

Cook's Tip
Sprinkling the cut surfaces of the banana with lemon juice keeps them from turning brown and also offsets the sweetness of the sauce.

SERVES 4-6

ORANGE PANCAKES

Try these on Pancake Day and you'll
decide they're far too good to save
for once a year!

120g/4oz plain flour
15ml/1 tbsp oil
1 whole egg
1 egg yolk
280ml/½ pint milk (or more)
Oil for frying
450g/1lb cream cheese or low fat soft cheese
120g/4oz sugar
Grated rind of 1 orange
60g/4 tbsps finely chopped nuts
140ml/¼ pint orange juice mixed with 10ml/2 tsps
    cornflour
4 oranges, peeled and segmented

1. Sift the flour into a mixing bowl and make a well in the centre.

2. Pour the oil, whole egg and egg yolk into the centre of the well and beat with a wooden spoon.

3. Gradually beat in the milk, incorporating the flour slowly. Set aside for 30 minutes.

4. Beat the cheese and sugar together with the orange rind until light and fluffy. Stir in the chopped nuts and set aside.

5. Heat a special crêpe pan or a frying pan and pour in a small amount of oil. Wipe over with a paper towel for a thin coating of oil on the bottom.

6. Pour a small amount of batter (about 30ml/2 tbsps) into the hot pan and swirl the batter to coat the base evenly. Pour out the excess to re-use.

7. Cook until the bottom is a light golden brown and turn over. Cook the other side and stack up the pancakes on a plate. Repeat with remaining batter to make 12 small or 6 large pancakes.

8. Spread some of the filling on the speckled side of each pancake and roll up or fold into triangles. Place in a warm oven while preparing the sauce.

9. Pour orange juice and cornflour mixture into a saucepan and bring to the boil, stirring constantly. Boil until thickened and clear. Stir in the orange segments. Spoon sauce over pancakes to serve.

Step 6 Pour batter into the hot pan and swirl to coat the base.

Step 7 When first side is brown, turn pancake over using a palette knife.

Cook's Notes

Time
Preparation takes about 30 minutes and cooking takes about 45 minutes. Prepare ahead of time and reheat about 15 minutes in a slow oven. Reheat sauce separately.

Variation
Use canned, pitted cherries as an alternative sauce. Hazelnuts, pecans or walnuts can be used.

Freezing
Unfilled pancakes can be stacked between sheets of non-stick or wax paper, placed in plastic bags and frozen for up to 3 months. Thaw at room temperature, separate and use with a variety of sweet or savoury fillings.

SERVES 4-6

MAPLE SYRUP MOUSSE

If you really want to splurge on a
special pudding, use pure maple syrup
instead of the flavoured kind.

4 eggs, separated
2 extra egg whites
180ml/6 fl oz maple flavoured syrup
280ml/½ pint double cream
Chopped pecans or walnuts to decorate

1. Place the syrup in a saucepan and bring to the boil. Continue boiling to reduce the syrup by one quarter.

2. Beat the egg yolks until thick and lemon coloured.

3. Pour the maple syrup onto the egg yolks in a thin, steady stream, beating with an electric mixer. Continue beating until the mixture has cooled.

4. Beat the egg whites until stiff but not dry and whip the cream until soft peaks form.

5. Fold the cream and egg whites into the maple mixture and spoon into a serving bowl or individual glasses. Refrigerate until slightly set and top with chopped walnuts or pecans to serve.

Step 3 Pour the hot syrup onto the beaten egg yolks in a thin, steady stream, beating constantly.

Step 5 Fold the cream and the egg whites into the maple mixture using a rubber spatula or large metal spoon.

Cook's Notes

 Time
Preparation takes about 30 minutes. It will take the syrup about 10 minutes to reduce.

 Variation
Although the hot syrup will "cook" the eggs, use powdered egg yolks and whites, if desired.

 Watchpoint
Be careful when boiling the syrup, since it can burn very easily.

MAKES 1 PIE

PUMPKIN PIE

Try this as a special autumn treat
when pumpkins are plentiful.

Pastry
120g/4oz plain flour
Pinch salt
60g/2oz butter, margarine or lard
Cold milk

Pumpkin Filling
450g/1lb cooked and mashed pumpkin
2 eggs
280ml/½ pint evaporated milk
120g/4oz brown sugar
5ml/1 tsp ground cinnamon
1.25ml/¼ tsp ground allspice
Pinch nutmeg
Pecan halves for decoration

Step 1 Add enough cold milk to bring the mixture together into a firm ball.

Step 3 Roll the pastry around a lightly-floured rolling pin and then lower it into the dish.

Step 1 Rub the fat into the flour until the mixture resembles fine breadcrumbs.

1. To prepare the pastry, sift the flour and a pinch of salt into a mixing bowl. Rub in the fat until the mixture resembles fine breadcrumbs. Stir in enough cold milk to bring the mixture together into a firm ball. Cover and chill for about 30 minutes before use.

2. Roll out the pastry on a lightly-floured surface to a circle about 28cm/11 inches in diameter.

3. Wrap the pastry around a lightly-floured rolling pin and lower it into a 25cm/10 inch round pie dish.

4. Press the pastry into the dish and flute the edge or crimp with a fork.

5. Prick the base lightly with the tines of a fork.

6. Combine all the filling ingredients in a mixing bowl and beat with an electric mixer until smooth. Alternatively, use a food processor. Pour into the pie crust and bake in a pre-heated 200°C/425°F/Gas Mark 7 oven. Bake for 10 minutes at this temperature and then lower the temperature to 180°C/350°F/Gas Mark 4 and bake for a further 40-50 minutes, or until the filling is set. Decorate with a circle of pecan halves.

Cook's Notes

Time
Preparation takes about 30 minutes and cooking takes about 50-60 minutes.

Cook's Tip
Pricking the base of the pastry lightly will prevent it from rising up in an air bubble in the middle of the pie.

Serving Ideas
Serve warm or cold with whipped cream.

MAKES 1 PIE

BLUEBERRY PIE

Blueberries are available frozen
from many large supermarkets,
but use fresh ones if you can.

Double quantity pastry for Pumpkin Pie recipe

Filling

450g/1lb blueberries
30g/2 tbsps cornflour
60ml/4 tbsps water
30ml/2 tbsps lemon juice
225g/8oz sugar
1 egg beaten with a pinch of salt

Step 4 Spoon the blueberry filling into the pastry-lined pie dish.

1. Prepare the pastry in the same way as for the Pumpkin Pie recipe.

2. Divide the pastry in half and roll out one half to form the base. Use a floured rolling pin to lower it into the dish, and press it against the sides. Chill the pastry in the dish and the remaining half of the pastry while preparing the filling.

3. Place the fruit in a bowl and mix the cornflour with the water and lemon juice. Pour it over the fruit, add the sugar and mix together gently.

4. Spoon the fruit filling into the pastry base.

5. Roll out the remaining pastry on a lightly-floured surface and cut it into strips.

6. Use the strips to make a lattice pattern on top of the filling and press the edges to stick them to the pastry base. Cut off any excess pastry.

7. Using your fingers or a fork, crimp the edges to decorate.

8. Brush the crimped edge of the pastry and the lattice strips lightly with the beaten egg and bake in a pre-heated 220°C/425°F/Gas Mark 7 oven for about 10 minutes. Reduce the heat to 180°C/350°F/Gas Mark 4 and bake for a further 40-45 minutes. Serve warm or cold.

Step 6 Cut strips of pastry and use to make a lattice pattern on top of the pie.

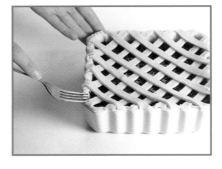

Step 7 Crimp by hand, or use a fork to make a decorative edge.

Cook's Notes

Time
Preparation takes about 30-40 minutes and cooking takes about 50-55 minutes.

Cook's Tip
Taste the blueberries before deciding how much sugar to add – it may not be necessary to add the full amount. If using frozen berries, drain them very well.

Variation
Other fruits such as raspberries, blackberries or blackcurrants may be used in the pie instead of blueberries.

ORANGE BREAD PUDDING

A light and luscious pudding with a spicy orange flavour.

1150ml/2 pints milk
8 slices white bread, crusts removed
60g/4 tbsps butter or margarine
6 egg yolks
3 egg whites
180g/6oz sugar
2.5ml/½ tsp freshly ground nutmeg
Pinch salt
120g/4oz orange marmalade

1. Heat the milk until just scalded.

2. In a large bowl, break the bread into cubes and add the butter. Stir in the hot milk until the butter is melted and the bread has broken up. Allow the mixture to cool to luke-warm.

3. Lightly grease a large soufflì dish or pudding basin.

4. Combine the egg yolks and whites in a bowl, and beat until frothy. Stir in the sugar, nutmeg and salt. Stir the egg mixture into the bread and milk mixture until just combined, and pour into the prepared mould.

5. Cover the mould with lightly greased foil and tie tightly. Place the dish on a rack in a large saucepan and fill with boiling water to within 2.5cm/1 inch of the top of the bowl.

6. Bring the water to boiling and then allow to simmer, covered, for 1½ hours, or until the pudding is firm in the centre.

7. Allow to cool for about 30 minutes and then loosen the edge with a knife. Invert onto a serving plate to unmould.

8. Spread the top with orange marmalade and serve warm or cold.

Step 4 Pour the pudding mixture into a lightly-greased mould. Pour to within about 2.5cm/1 inch of the top of the mould.

Step 7 When the pudding has cooled slightly, loosen the edge with a knife.

Step 8 Place a plate on top and then turn the pudding over to unmould.

Cook's Notes

Time
Preparation takes about 30 minutes and cooking takes about 1½ hours.

Cook's Tip
If serving the pudding cold, loosen the edge and then allow it to cool completely in the mould before unmoulding. This makes turning the pudding out a lot easier.

Watchpoint
Carefully check the level of water in the kettle at intervals. Do not allow the pudding to boil dry.

SERVES 4

MANGO AND COCONUT WITH LIME SAUCE

The taste of mango with lime is sensational, especially when served with the deliciously creamy sauce in this stylish dessert.

2 large, ripe mangoes, peeled and sliced
1 fresh coconut
2 egg yolks
60g/4 tbsps sugar
Juice and grated rind of 2 limes
140ml/¼ pint double cream, whipped

Step 3 Whisk egg yolks and sugar until thick and light lemon in colour.

1. Arrange thin slices of mango on plates.

2. Break coconut in half and then into smaller sections. Grate the white pulp, taking care to avoid grating the brown skin. Use the coarse side of the grater to make shreds and scatter them over the mango slices.

3. Place egg yolks and sugar in the top of a double boiler or a large bowl. Whisk until very thick and lemon coloured.

4. Stir in the lime juice and place mixture over simmering water. Whisk constantly while the mixture gently cooks and becomes thick and creamy.

5. Remove from the heat and place in another bowl of iced water to cool quickly. Whisk the mixture while it cools.

6. Fold in the whipped cream and spoon onto the fruit. Garnish with the grated lime rind.

Cook's Notes

 Time
Preparation takes about 40 minutes and cooking takes about 8 minutes.

 Preparation
The sauce can be chilled for up to 30 minutes. After that, it may start to separate.

 Variation
Serve the sauce with other fruit such as papayas, peaches, pineapple or berries.

Watchpoint
It is important that the water under the sauce does not boil. If it does, it can cause curdling or cook the mixture too quickly, resulting in a poor texture.

SERVES 4

SUNBURST ORANGES

Sunny oranges look and
taste beautiful in a rosy red sauce
made with red wine.

4 large oranges
225g/8oz sugar
90ml/6 tbsps water
140ml/¼ pint full-bodied red wine

Step 1 Trim the rough edges of the orange peel and then cut the peel into thin strips.

1. Using a swivel vegetable peeler, remove just the peel from the oranges. Be sure not to take off any white pith. Cut the peel into very thin strips.

2. Peel off the pith from the oranges using a small serrated knife. Take off the pith in thin strips to preserve the shape of the fruit. Peel the oranges over a bowl to catch any juice. Slice the fruit thinly and place in a bowl or on serving plates.

3. Place the sugar and water in a heavy-based saucepan over very low heat. Cook very slowly until the sugar dissolves completely and forms a thin syrup.

4. Add the strips of peel and boil rapidly for 2 minutes. Do not allow the syrup to brown. Remove the peel with a draining spoon and place on a lightly oiled plate to cool. Cool the syrup slightly and then pour in the wine. If the syrup hardens, heat very gently, stirring to dissolve again. Allow the syrup to cool completely.

5. Spoon the syrup over the oranges and arrange the peel on top to serve.

Cook's Notes

 Time
Preparation takes about 40 minutes. The syrup will take about 1 hour to cool completely.

Cook's Tip
Add any juice collected while peeling the oranges to the syrup for extra flavour.

 Watchpoint
Do not pour warm syrup over the oranges as they will cook.

SERVES 6

PERSIMMON PUDDINGS

Rich and satisfying puddings for autumn
made with plump, bright orange persimmons or Sharon fruit.
Spice them up with preserved or fresh ginger.

2-4 ripe persimmons or Sharon fruit (depending on size)
60ml/4 tbsps honey
Juice and rind of 1 small orange
1 egg
140ml/¼ pint single cream
90g/3oz plain flour
2.5ml/½ tsp baking powder
2.5ml/½ tsp baking soda
Pinch cinnamon and nutmeg
30g/2 tbsps melted butter
1 small piece preserved ginger, finely chopped, or small piece freshly grated ginger
60g/4 tbsps chopped walnuts or pecans
Whipped cream, orange segments and walnut or pecan halves to garnish

Orange sauce

280ml/½ pint orange juice
Sugar to taste
15ml/1 tbsp cornflour

1. Peel the persimmons or Sharon fruit by dropping them into boiling water for about 5 seconds. Remove to a bowl of cold water and leave to stand briefly. This treatment makes the peels easier to remove.

2. Scoop out any seeds and purée the fruit until smooth. Add the honey, orange juice and rind, egg and cream, and process once or twice. Pour the mixture into a bowl.

3. Sift the flour, baking powder, baking soda and spices over the persimmon purée and gradually fold together. Stir in the melted butter, ginger and nuts and spoon into well buttered ramekin dishes. Place in a bain marie and bake until risen and set, about 45 minutes, in a pre-heated 180°C/350°F/Gas Mark 4 oven. Test by inserting a skewer into the middle. If the skewer comes out clean the puddings are set. Allow to cool slightly.

4. Combine the sauce ingredients and cook slowly, stirring continuously, until thickened and cleared.

5. When the puddings have cooled slightly, loosen them from the edge of the dish and turn out onto a plate. Spoon some of the sauce over each and garnish with whipped cream, orange segments and nuts.

Step 3 Gradually fold the dry ingredients in the persimmon purée using a large metal spoon or a rubber spatula.

Step 5 Spoon some of the sauce over each pudding to glaze it.

Cook's Notes

Time
Preparation takes about 25 minutes and cooking takes about 45 minutes.

Serving Ideas
The pudding and sauce may be served warm or cold. If serving cold, cut the quantity of cornflour down to 10ml or 2 tsps, as the sauce will thicken on standing.

Cook's Tip
To prevent a skin from forming on top of a dessert sauce, sprinkle lightly with sugar to cover the top completely. If using this method, adjust the quantity of sugar in the recipe.

SERVES 6

PEARS IN RED WINE

Red wine and cinnamon complement pears
beautifully. Add a garnish of crisp almonds
for this easy-to-make French classic.

850ml/1½ pints dry red wine
225g/8oz sugar
1 cinnamon stick
1 strip lemon peel
6 William or Comice pears, even sized
60g/4 tbsps flaked almonds
15g/1 tbsp cornflour mixed with 45ml/3 tbsps water
Mint leaves to garnish

1. Pour the wine into a deep saucepan that will hold 6 pears standing upright.

2. Add the sugar, cinnamon and lemon peel, and bring to the boil slowly to dissolve the sugar. Stir occasionally.

3. Peel pears, remove 'eye' on the bottom, but leave on the stems.

4. Stand the pears close together in the wine, so that they remain standing. Cover the pan and poach gently over low heat for about 25-35 minutes, or until tender. If the wine does not cover the pears completely, baste the tops frequently as they cook.

5. Meanwhile, toast almonds on a baking sheet in a moderate oven for about 8-10 minutes, stirring them occasionally for even browning. Remove and allow to cool.

6. When pears are cooked, remove from the liquid to a serving dish. Boil the liquid to reduce it by about half. If it is still too thin to coat the pears, thicken it with 15ml/1 tbsp cornflour dissolved in 45ml/3 tbsps water.

7. Pour syrup over the pears and sprinkle with almonds. Serve warm or refrigerate until lightly chilled. Garnish pears with mint leaves at the stems just before serving.

Step 3 Peel pears and remove the 'eye' on the base of each.

Step 4 Stand the pears upright in the saucepan.

Step 7 The syrup should be thick enough to coat the pears lightly.

Cook's Notes

Time
Preparation takes about 25 minutes and cooking takes about 50 minutes.

Variation
Use white wine to poach the pears, and flavour with cinnamon or a vanilla pod.

Serving Ideas
Add whipped cream, ice cream or custard for a richer pudding

SERVES 6

SWEET POTATO PUDDING

Sweet potatoes are becoming increasingly
popular. This particular recipe makes
an unusual savoury side dish.

2 medium-size sweet potatoes
570ml/1 pint milk
2 eggs
180g/6oz sugar
5ml/1 tsp cinnamon
30g/1oz pecans or walnuts, roughly chopped
30g/2 tbsps butter
90ml/6 tbsps whisky

Step 2 When the egg and sugar mixture is light and fluffy, combine it with cinnamon and pecans and add to the potato and milk mixture.

Step 3 Pour the mixture into a lightly-buttered shallow baking dish and dot with the remaining butter.

Step 4 Pour the bourbon over the baked pudding just before serving.

1. Peel the potatoes and grate them coarsely. Combine with the milk.

2. Beat the eggs and gradually add the sugar, continuing until light and fluffy. Combine with the cinnamon and the nuts.

3. Stir into the potatoes and milk and pour the mixture into a lightly buttered shallow baking dish. Dot with the remaining butter.

4. Bake about 45 minutes to 1 hour in a pre-heated 180°C/350°F Gas Mark 4 oven. Bake until the pudding is set and then pour over the whisky just before serving.

Cook's Notes

Time
Preparation takes about 25 minutes and cooking takes 45 minutes to 1 hour.

Serving Ideas
While this pudding is usually served as a savoury accompaniment to poultry or ham, it can also be served as a sweet pudding with whipped cream or ice cream.

SERVES 6-8

STAINED GLASS DESSERT

Named for the effect of the cubes of colourful gelatine in the filling, this pretty and light pudding can be made well in advance of serving.

90g/3oz each of three fruit-flavoured gelatine (assorted)
1 package digestive biscuits
90g/6 tbsps sugar
120g/4oz butter or margarine
45g/3 tbsps unflavoured gelatine
60ml/4 tbsps cold water
3 eggs, separated
90g/6 tbsps sugar
120g/4oz cream cheese
Juice and rind of 1 large lemon
120ml/4 fl oz whipping cream

1. Prepare the flavoured gelatines according to package directions.

2. Pour into 3 shallow pans and refrigerate until firm.

3. Crush the biscuits in a food processor with the sugar. Pour melted butter through the funnel with the machine running to blend thoroughly.

4. Press half the mixture into a 20cm/8 inch springform pan lined with greaseproof paper. Refrigerate until firm. Reserve half the mixture for topping.

5. Sprinkle the gelatine onto the water in a small saucepan and allow to stand until spongy. Heat gently until the gelatine dissolves and the liquid is clear. Combine the egg yolks, lemon juice and sugar and beat until slightly thickened. Beat in the cream cheese a bit at a time. Pour in the gelatine in a thin, steady stream, beating constantly. Allow to stand, stirring occasionally until beginning to thicken. Place in a bowl of ice water to speed up the setting process.

6. Whip the cream until soft. Whip the egg whites until stiff peaks form and fold both the cream and the egg whites into the lemon-cream cheese mixture when the gelatine has begun to thicken.

7. Cut the flavoured gelatines into cubes and fold carefully into the cream cheese mixture.

8. Pour onto the prepared crust. Sprinkle the remaining crust mixture on top, pressing down very carefully.

9. Chill overnight in the refrigerator. Loose the mixture carefully from the sides of the pan, open the pan and unmould. Slice or spoon out to serve.

Step 7 Fold the cubes of unflavoured gelatine carefully into the lemon cheese mixture using a rubber spatula.

Step 8 Sprinkle reserved crumb topping carefully over the mixture and press down lightly.

Cook's Notes

Time
Preparation takes about 35-40 minutes. Flavoured gelatines will take about 1-1½ hours to set, and the finished cake must be refrigerated overnight.

Preparation
Dessert may be prepared a day or two in advance and kept in the refrigerator. Do not keep longer than 2 days.

Variation
Use orange juice or lime juice instead of lemon. Alternatively, soak the gelatine in water and use vanilla essence to flavour the cream cheese mixture.

SERVES 6

LEMON FLAN

A tangy lemon filling with the surprising
crunch of cornmeal make this a very
special pudding.

180g/6oz plain flour
Pinch salt and sugar
90g/6 tbsps butter or margarine
30g/2 tbsps plus 5g/1 tsp vegetable shortening
60-75ml/4-5 tbsps cold water

Filling
60g/4 tbsps softened butter
225g/8oz sugar
3-4 eggs, depending on size
15g/1 tbsp yellow cornmeal
Rind and juice of 1 lemon

Step 9 Lift the pastry around the rolling pin and carefully unroll to lower it into the dish.

1. Sift the flour, salt and sugar into a bowl or process once or twice in a food processor.

2. Add the butter or margarine and shortening and rub into the flour until the mixture resembles fine breadcrumbs, or use the food processor.

3. Add enough water to bring the mixture together in a firm dough. Knead lightly to eliminate cracks, wrap and chill for 30 minutes while preparing the filling.

4. Cream the butter with the sugar until the sugar dissolves.

5. Add the eggs, one at a time, beating well in between each addition.

6. Stir in the cornmeal, rind and juice of the lemon.

7. Roll out the pastry in a circle on a well-floured surface.

8. Roll the pastry carefully onto the rolling pin and transfer to a 20cm/9 inch pie or flan dish.

9. Lower the pastry carefully into the dish and press against the sides and base. Roll over the rim of the flan dish with the rolling pin to cut off the excess pastry.

10. Pour in the filling and bake at 180°C/350°F/Gas Mark 4 for about 45 minutes. Lower the temperature to 170°C/325°F/Gas Mark 3 if the flan begins to brown too quickly. Cook until the filling sets. Allow to cool completely before serving. Sprinkle lightly with icing sugar before cutting, if desired.

Step 10 Pour the filling evenly over the base of the unbaked pastry.

Cook's Notes

 Time
Preparation takes about 30 minutes and cooking takes about 45 minutes.

 Freezing
The flan may be frozen uncooked. Open freeze in the dish and when firm, wrap well and freeze for up to 3 months. Defrost at room temperature and then bake according to the recipe directions.

 Serving Ideas
Lemon flan may be served with whipped cream.
Decorate the edge with lemon slices, if desired.

MAKES 1 PIE

MOCHA ICE CREAM PIE

Unbelievably simple, yet incredibly
delicious and impressive, this is a perfect
ending to a summer meal or a spicy one anytime.

12 Digestive biscuits, crushed
90g/3oz butter or margarine, melted
840ml/1½ pints coffee ice cream
60g/2oz plain chocolate, melted
120g/4oz flaked coconut

1. Crush biscuits with a rolling pin or in a food processor. Mix with melted butter or margarine.

2. Press into an 8½ inch spring form tin. Chill thoroughly in the refrigerator.

3. Meanwhile, combine 4 tbsps coconut with the melted chocolate. When cooled but not solidified, add about a quarter of the coffee ice cream, mixing well.

4. Spread the mixture on the base of a crust and freeze until firm.

5. Soften the remaining ice cream with an electric mixer or food processor and spread over the chocolate-coconut layer. Re-freeze until firm.

6. Toast the remaining coconut in a moderate oven, stirring frequently until pale golden brown. Allow to cool completely.

7. Remove the pie from the freezer and leave in the refrigerator 30 minutes before serving. Push up the base of the dish and place the pie on a serving plate. Sprinkle the top with toasted coconut. Cut into wedges to serve.

Step 2 Press the crust mixture into the base and up the sides of a flan dish.

Step 4 Spread the chocolate-coconut mixture evenly over the bottom of the crust.

Step 5 Spread the coffee ice cream carefully over the chocolate-coconut layer and re-freeze.

Cook's Notes

Time
Preparation takes about 25 minutes. The ice cream will take several hours to freeze.

Freezing
The pie may be prepared well in advance and kept in the freezer for up to 3 months. Coconut may be sprinkled on top before freezing or just before serving.

Variation
If desired, use vanilla ice cream in place of the coffee.

MAKES 850ml/1½ pints

GUAVA MINT SORBET

When a light dessert is called for, a
sorbet can't be surpassed. The exotic
taste of guava works well with mint.

4 ripe guavas
180g/6oz granulated sugar
280ml/½ pint water
30g/2 tbsps chopped fresh mint
1 lime
1 egg white
Fresh mint leaves for garnish

Step 4 Process the frozen mixture again and gradually work in the egg white.

Step 2 Combine the puréed guava, mint and cold syrup.

Step 3 Freeze the mixture until slushy and then process to break up the ice crystals.

1. Combine the sugar and water in a heavy-based saucepan and bring slowly to the boil to dissolve the sugar. When the mixture is a clear syrup, boil rapidly for 30 seconds. Allow to cool to room temperature and then chill in the refrigerator.

2. Cut the guavas in half and scoop out the pulp. Discard the peels and seeds and purée the fruit until smooth in a food processor. Add the mint and combine with cold syrup. Add lime juice until the right balance of sweetness is reached.

3. Pour the mixture into a shallow container and freeze until slushy. Process again to break up ice crystals and then freeze until firm.

4. Whip the egg white until stiff but not dry. Process the sorbet again and when smooth, add the egg white. Mix once or twice and then freeze again until firm.

5. Remove from the freezer 15 minutes before serving and keep in the refrigerator.

6. Scoop out and garnish each serving with mint leaves.

Cook's Notes

Time
Preparation takes about 2-3 hours, allowing the sorbet to freeze in between processing.

Preparation
If a food processor is not available, use an electric mixer.

Freezing
The sorbet will keep in the freezer for up to 3 months in a well-sealed, rigid container.

MAKES 10

FRUIT TURNOVERS

Use bought shortcrust pastry,
either fresh or frozen to
make this recipe easy.

450g/1lb Shortcrust pastry
10 ripe fresh apricots, halved and stoned, or 450g/1lb
    canned apricots, well drained
450g/1lb cream cheese
Oil for deep frying
Icing sugar

Step 3 Place the cheese and apricots on the lower half of each tortilla.

1. Roll out pastry and cut into even size rounds. Heat oil in a deep saucepan, sauté pan or deep-fat fryer to a depth of at least 5cm/2 inches. Oil should reach a temperature of 190°C/375°F.

2. Cut the apricots into quarters and the cheese into 10 even pieces.

3. Place one piece of cheese and an even amount of apricots on the lower half of each pastry round. Fold over the upper half and seal the edges. Crimp tightly into a decorative pattern.

4. Fry 1 turnover at a time until golden on both sides. Baste the upper side frequently with oil.

5. Drain well on paper towels and serve warm, sprinkled with icing sugar.

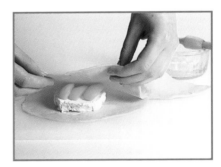

Step 3 Fold over the upper half and seal the edges.

Step 3 Crimp the edges tightly into a decorative pattern.

Cook's Notes

Time
Preparation takes about 40 minutes-1 hour for the tortillas and about 20 minutes to prepare the rest of the dish.

Variation
Other fruit may be used in the empanadas instead of apricots. Substitute fresh guava, mango or papaya cut into short strips. Sliced peaches may also be used as well as cherries, although they are not native to the Southwest.

Preparation
As with all deep-fried foods, fruit empanadas are best served as soon as they are cooked.

SERVES 6

FROZEN LIME AND BLACKCURRANT CREAM

An impressive pudding that's perfect
for entertaining because it can
be made well in advance.

Juice and rind of 4 limes
Water
225g/8oz sugar
120g/4oz blackcurrants
3 egg whites
280ml/½ pint double cream, whipped

Step 3 Boil the lime juice, water and sugar rapidly once a clear syrup forms.

1. Measure the lime juice and make up to 90ml/3 fl oz with water if necessary.

2. Combine with the sugar in a heavy-based pan and bring to the boil slowly to dissolve the sugar.

3. When the mixture forms a clear syrup, boil rapidly to 130°C/250°F on a sugar thermometer.

4. Meanwhile, combine the blackcurrants with about 60ml/4 tbsps water in a small saucepan. Bring to the boil and then simmer, covered, until very soft. Purée, sieve to remove the seeds and skin, and set aside to cool.

5. Whisk the egg whites until stiff but not dry and then pour on the hot sugar syrup in a steady stream, whisking constantly. Add the lime rind and allow the meringue to cool.

6. When cold, fold in the whipped cream. Pour in the purée and marble through the mixture with a rubber spatula. Do not over-fold. Pour the mixture into a lightly-oiled mould or bowl and freeze until firm. Leave 30 minutes in the refrigerator before serving or dip the mould for about 10 seconds in hot water. Place a plate over the bottom of the mould, invert and shake to turn out. Garnish with extra whipped cream and lime slices.

Step 3 Pour the syrup gradually onto the whisked egg whites, beating constantly.

Step 6 Fold the cream and the fruit purée into the egg whites, marbling the purée through the mixture.

Cook's Notes

 Time
Preparation takes about 40 minutes. The cream should be left in the freezer overnight to firm completely.

Variation
Substitute 2 large or 3 medium lemons for the limes. Other berries, such as raspberries, blackberries, or red currants, may be substituted for the blackcurrants.

 Freezing
The cream will keep in its mould, well covered, in the freezer for up to 2 months. Remove from the freezer and leave in the refrigerator for 30 minutes or dip in hot water as the recipe suggests.

INDEX